BOOK OF
Designer
Gardens

Words: Celia Haddon
Photographs: Roy Botterell

SUNDAY EXPRESS BOOK OF DESIGNER GARDENS
Designer: Geoff Staff

Designed and produced by Parke Sutton Limited, 8 Thorpe Road,
Norwich NR1 1RY for Jarrold Colour Publications,
Barrack Street, Norwich NR3 1TR

Photographs on pages 26 and 27
by courtesy of the National Trust

ISBN 0 7117 0500 3

BOOK OF
Designer Gardens

SUNDAY
EXPRESS
magazine

Words: Celia Haddon
Photographs: Roy Botterell

JARROLD

Contents

Introduction

Garden designers, in trying to create order and beauty out of chaos, have the best of examples to follow. 'God Almighty first planted a garden. And indeed, it is the purest of human pleasures. It is the greatest refreshment to the spirits of man; without which buildings and palaces are but gross handyworks,' wrote Francis Bacon some four centuries ago.

Gardening, he went on to point out, was more difficult than just mere building. 'When ages grow to civility and elegance, men come to build stately soon than to garden finely.' A good argument, one can't help feeling, for calling in not just the professional architect but the professional garden designer. Some of us amateurs will never garden finely until we are humble enough to realise that we may need some help. Yet somehow there remains a feeling that while it is quite acceptable to call in an interior designer, designing the exterior is something different. Indeed, the whole idea of applying design, at all, to gardens still needs to be emphasised. Many people still believe that gardens are just where you grow a lot of plants regardless of the overall effect.

Calling in a garden designer need not be a confession of incompetence, so much as a step towards more enjoyment in the garden. Garden design in Britain has never been so alive – both

● **A view of Anthony du Gard Pasley's house and Edwardian-style garden.**

with ideas and with men and women who have chosen the profession. The twelve garden designers in this book display, not just professional ability of a high order, but also an impressive variety of styles and talents. All twelve also love plants and gardens.

The twelve designers in this book are at the top of their profession, which has now become a fashionable occupation. True, there are probably more mediocre, even unskilled, garden designers than ever before, but nevertheless the resurgence of the profession is part of the optimism of the 1990s. To create, or to find somebody to create for you, a beautiful garden is to put your faith in the future – a future which no longer looks as gloomy as it did a couple of decades ago.

Gardening is again taking its place as *the* English art. The Prince of Wales, following in the tradition of a gardening family, has lovingly created a beautiful garden in Gloucestershire. Chelsea Flower Show has become so crowded that numbers have to be limited by advance booking. Garden centre retailing is finally moving into the big time. No wonder then that garden designing is all the rage. At worst, the garden designer may simply be another name for the jobbing gardener, useful for the heavy work but without taste or skill. Those who are unlucky enough to hire the less skilled can find themselves left with dull design and a lot of plants, hastily put in, which slowly die in the following year.

Against this background then, the professional expertise, the training and the years of experience of the real garden designer need reasserting. Designing a good garden is a difficult task – a very difficult task. It requires so many skills – the designer's eye to see the garden as a whole, the intimate experience and knowledge of a huge range of plants, empathy with clients who may not be able to put into words what is wanted for the garden, the foresight to envisage not just the garden's coming of age in 10 years time, but also the client's ability (financial or otherwise) to maintain it, and finally that great talent, the capacity to work within a limited budget.

What is exciting about garden design in Britain today is the sheer diversity of styles and talents. It is for this diversity that these twelve designers were chosen. We are not confined to one gardening style, thank goodness, though the judges at Chelsea Flower show in some years give this impression. This is not to say that any of the twelve designers in this book are rigidly confined to one style. All of them are able enough to carry out a client's instructions even when what is required might not be their own personal choice of a garden. All enjoy changing styles to fit the garden. Yet each has a style of their own.

This they display in their own gardens. For this book is not about designer gardens in general, but about designer gardens in particular – gardens created for their own pleasure, for their own use, and only secondarily as laboratories where they can try out ideas. The pictures show the garden designer at home. These are women and men who love gardens so much that while their work is gardening, so is their leisure. This is not as common as you might think. In the course of selecting 12 garden designers, I discovered that a surprising number relaxed at home surrounded by bare fields, concrete paving or just a messy back garden not fit for the photographer. Understandably for some, working on gardens all day meant they did not wish to work on their own gardens in their free time. It shows a real love of gardening to spend both working and leisure time in the garden.

The profession of gardening design goes back a long way. We begin to know the names of gardeners in Tudor times. The Elizabethan herbalists who classified and documented garden flowers and herbs and the Tradescant family who were responsible for bringing in many new plants, began to create a science of horticulture. Garden designs were born in the early books which gave plans for knot gardens.

But it was in the eighteenth century that the garden designer came into his own. His canvas was the whole countryside. 'Why may not a whole estate be thrown into a kind of garden by frequent plantations?' wrote the essayist Joseph Addison. The great landowners of the time transformed not so much the garden, as the whole landscape round their houses – diverting rivers, making lakes, even building artificial hills. No longer was the garden sharply cut off from nature – nature herself had become the garden.

The landscape designer Charles Bridgeman borrowed the surrounding landscape for his gardens by using the ha-ha, an invisible ditch which kept out animals from the surrounding farmland without spoiling the view. His contemporary William Kent laid it down that 'all gardening is landscape painting.' Their successor Capability (Lancelot) Brown developed this approach into what was literally the landscape garden. Both the views into the house in its parkland and the views from the house outward must be picturesque – the result of careful design using architectural features such as lakes, bridges, hillsides and temples. These features existed because the design required them. A bridge might lead nowhere: but if it improved the view, then a bridge would be built.

In Britain this scale of landscape design survives only in the public sector – reduced often to the diminution of visual harm, rather than the enhancement of beauty. Landscape designers and garden designers today follow two different professions. A few garden designers are landscape architects too, but many landscape architects have never designed a garden. Garden designers, on the whole, are working within smaller spaces and with far less money. It is rare (though not unknown) that a private client can afford to dam a stream or build an artificial hill. It is rare also for a client to plan, not for his own generation, but for genera-

tions to come. Capability Brown thought nothing of designing his landscapes with trees that would take two generations to develop their full beauty. In today's world of social change who would dare to suppose that a garden will stay in the same family for a century or more?

The Victorian rich of the next generation fell in love with the greenhouse and the astounding richness of foreign flower and colour that it could supply. The art of elaborate bedding schemes survives in the seaside floral clock, the elaborate carpet fantasies of boroughs like Torbay, and in the flowerbeds of large parks. It is still practised with verve and skill by tens of thousands of dedicated small gardeners. For it is a surprisingly low-maintenance style of gardening, requiring a lot of greenhouse space, immense effort in the spring but little else all through the summer. But it is a gardening style that has fallen down the social scale – an art of the small backyard or the cramped suburban garden rather than the country house. It is to my regret that I failed to discover a talented garden designer who uses this style in all its old glory.

Today's most common gardening tradition goes back to the Victorian writer, William Robinson, who argued against the elaborate geometry of Victorian gardens in favour of the natural style using hardy plants, rather than exotics which had to be taken into the greenhouse each winter. Bedding out schemes gave way to herbaceous borders. More directly influential today is Gertrude Jekyll, a painter who turned to garden design-

ing with the unusual motivation of finding something she could do as she became more and more shortsighted. Not only are many Jekyll gardens open to the public but most of her books are still in print.

Gertrude Jekyll's influence is a living one. One of the designers in this book, Michael Balston, told me that his inspiration comes from this particular passage in one of her books:- 'I am strongly of the opinion that the possession of a quantity of plants, however good the plants may be themselves and however ample their number, does not make a garden: it only makes a collection. Having got the plants the great thing is to use them with careful selection and definite intention.'

It was the blend of informality of planting and formality of design which made Gertrude Jekyll in partnership with the architect Edwin Lutyens so influential. His was the underlying 'hard' design of paths, walls and shape. 'Every garden scheme,' he wrote, 'should have a backbone, a central ideal beautifully phrased. Every wall, path, stone and flower should have its relationship to the central design.' This design was then clothed in plants by Gertrude Jekyll, who paid particular attention to colour and plant associations.

Between the wars and since, the influence of Lawrence Johnston at Hidcote Manor in the Cotswolds and Vita Sackville-West at Sissinghurst in Kent has been pre-eminent. Their gardens are visited by tens of thousands of people yearly and their ideas, sometimes even the minutiae of their planting, are widely imitated. I have been invited to admire a white border or a Hidcote red border more often than I care to remember, sometimes in quite inappropriate places like the tiny backyard of a small London terraced house. Such moments make one grateful for the existence of the professional garden designer, who will caution against the folly of inappropriate imitation.

Nevertheless this particular tradition is still probably what most people desire – herbaceous borders, dizzily romantic roses, and an artifice concealed by an air of natural beauty. The idea of the simple cottage garden with its borders crammed with old fashioned favourites is a powerful one. There is now a Cottage Garden Society and the cottage garden look triumphs at Chelsea Flower show perhaps more often than it should. Nostalgia for a past that never happened – most cottage gardens would have been full of vegetables rather than flowers – lives on in the garden. Many of the designers I interviewed have much enjoyed creating modern gardens but find that most of their clients do not want a modern approach. 'I get the impression that people think of gardens as a refuge from the modern things in life. They are seeking reassurance in the garden, so the design regrettably sometimes tends to be backward looking.' said Michael Balston. Despite a note of regret in his voice, his own garden with its lawns, perennial flowers and summerhouse is no exception.

In its careful reconstruction of country house gardens, the National Trust has had a great influence on gardeners. Garden visiting has become an important feature of the fine weekend for many of us – thanks to the National Trust's policy of careful reconstruction of gardens. The lure of the past is in part due to the Trust's care and skill. As chief gardens adviser to the National Trust John Sales, one of the people featured in this book, keeps a designer's eye on 110 gardens, fifty landscape parks, various other cultivated areas and twenty-six national plant collections. He is responsible for making and keeping all their gardens and parks attractive. Some 350 gardeners work for the Trust under him and with the help of three assistants each of the 110 gardens must be visited yearly. The Trust's gardens exert a huge influence on gardeners everywhere. It is surprising that he finds time to garden at all, yet his own garden is in the natural tradition of lawns, herbaceous borders, and interesting plants.

The large country garden is not just a pleasure of the past. It is still possible to find gardeners willing to reshape a lake or alter a hillside. Arabella Lennox-Boyd has done just this in transforming a Victorian house overshadowed by gloomy rhododendrons and laurels into a romantic fantasy, set in a garden where old fashioned roses and sweet peas pour their fragrance over the stone terraces.

If at times the modern movement seems to have passed gardens by, it is because the British still value prettiness and romance in the garden. Gardens are perhaps the one area where the often philistine British can allow themselves to value beauty. And the language of the garden is the secret language of the British heart – surprisingly tender, nostalgic, and romantic. Mark Rumary, who for the past 27 years has been designing gardens for Notcutts, the Suffolk nursery firm follows this tradition. His

● **John Sales uses traditional plants in herbaceous borders.**

garden shows that the Jekyll methods of planting can be applied in a relatively small space without difficulties of scale. There is a modesty and restraint about his own garden which makes it a little gem. One of my happiest memories of the summer of 1988 was sitting having afternoon tea, with currant loaf and cake, in his garden.

For if the garden is a refuge, the little bit of paradise which is far from the fears and stresses outside world, do we have any right to object? Is it not understandable that we should feel nostalgia for a vanished world – a golden age secure from the violence and the hard-faced moneymaking of the world in the 1990s? Certainly Antony du Gard Pasley has chosen to create for himself a garden that has turned its back on the modern world. 'I was determined to make the garden look back to 1910, the days before the First World War' he declared. As an enthusiast for the Mapp and Lucia novels of E.F. Benson, the idea of an Edwardian atmosphere pleases him. In true Jekyll style, he has created various garden 'rooms' – a winter garden at the dark side of the house, a garden of sunlight yellows in front, and a main garden full of silvery greys, pale pinks and mauves and muted blues.

The English have a passion, not just for gardens but also for individual plants. Susan Gernaey's garden is proof of this. In unpromising surroundings, a little back garden in Battersea, she has successfully captured the *rus in urbe* look, thanks to her intense care for her plants. She has also brought this passion into the con-

servatory – perhaps the most successful way of achieving not an outdoor room but an indoor garden. Her expertise in both design and plants is much needed now that the British have rediscovered the conservatory. As she says: 'The most common mistake is to assume that plants like the same conditions as people. They don't. So those glass extensions which are just part of the living room aren't necessarily good for growing plants.'

Plantsmanship is also required by those who work in difficult surroundings. Iris Strachan, an example of the Scottish skill in gardening which has made the Scottish head gardener a byword in fact and fiction, also follows the *rus in urbe* tradition. In her Edinburgh back garden she keeps rare plants. For she was one of the first Scots to see the need for plant conservation and is committed to helping rescue the old varieties. She was one of the first members of the National Council for the Conservation of Plants and Gardens and heads the local group.

Even more impressive is her garden in Broughton, Peeblesshire, Scotland. It is the coldest and highest county in Britain with the possibility of frost every single month of the year. Snow can fall as late as June and the wind can be gale force 9. Hers is what she calls 'a garden of thugs' – plants that would be horribly rampant and invasive down South are strong enough to survive. 'Living in the coldest spot in Scotland, as I do, has been a great help in designing Scottish gardens,' she explains with understatement.

There is also an impressive natural quality. In some parts of her Peeblesshire garden she uses a technique of planting strong perennial plants into the grass, then using a mower to define the border between lawn and flowers. Iris Strachan's oriental poppies growing out of the long grass are simply magic.

It would be wrong to make too violent a distinction between those designers whose primary passion is plants and those whose primary interest is design. The English love of plants grows on even those who are conscious of its potential for harming design. John Brookes was the rebel of the 1960s, the designer who argued that the garden should not be primarily a place for growing plants but an outdoor room for human beings to live in. 'The essence of a John Brookes garden is the contrast between geometry and nature – but that's the essence of any successful garden,' said a professor of landscape architecture in California.

John Brookes turned his formidable skill to the small garden well before Chelsea Flower show had even acknowledged its existence. 'The garden is a place primarily for *people,*' he declared and unlike many designers of the time he recognised that people included not only keen gardeners with a lot of money and time, but keen gardeners without time or money or just people who didn't want to garden much. Thanks to this realism and to a constant stream of well written explicative books his influence on ordinary gardeners has been immense. His is a refreshing and liberating voice, reminding the garden owner that gardens can be used and enjoyed even by those who do not wish to spend hours gardening. The idle gardener, if he reads John Brookes, can nevertheless achieve a pleasantly designed garden.

However, John Brookes himself is far from idle. He is a passionate gardener. Not for him the small back yard with one specimen tree and only a few foliage plants. He is in love with plants, particularly with interestingly shaped foliage plants. Denmans, the garden made by Mrs Joyce Robinson, and from which he runs the Clock House School of Gardening Design is a real gardener's garden – full of the most extraordinary plants growing in comparitive wildness. Perhaps because of his love of foliage and shape rather than colour John Brookes is also enthusiastic about using herbs to beautify the garden.

Now that the green movement has become so popular, it is no wonder that herbs are increasingly to be found in a garden for their culinary virtues, their hospitality to bees and their fragrance. Foliage, rather than just mere flowers, is now popular too and herbs with their modest little flowers have their own intrinsic beauty of foliage and form. Simon and Judith Hopkinson, of Hollington Herbs, have played their part in promoting herb gardening. Their herb garden designs, particularly the knot garden designs, feed a greater nostalgia – for a past 400 years back where a garden was the place not just for beauty but for use and where the same plant could be enjoyed for its beauty and used for its medicinal virtues.

The garden of Anthony Paul owes no evident debt to the past. Not for him the piety of Jekyll worship or search for good taste: he has struck out in a new direction unfettered by the past. 'We English are constipated by our forefathers. We all copy the past in our gardens. I think we should look at new ideas and new concepts. With modern buildings we should match our landscapes to them. We've done it with interiors, why, not exteriors?'

His own garden is six-and-a-half acres of lakes, streams, woodland and vistas with not a rhododendron in sight. 'I don't like rhododendrons anyway' It is a wild theatrical garden, and like Iris Strachan he plants perennials within grass, and uses the mower to distinguish between lawn and border. With flamboyant plants like *Gunnera manicata,* and great swathes of round-leaved *Peltiphyllum peltatum, Petasites hybridus,* the native butterbur and its Asian cousin, *Petasites japonicus,* his garden is – there is no other word so accurate – fun.

Myles Challis shares his taste for exotic though hardy plants with Anthony Paul. In a small backyard in East London he has chosen to recreate a fantastic tropical jungle with soft forest floor, tall shrubs and exotic foliage. His collection of outdoor exotics – hardy plants with foliage and sometimes flowers that *look* tropical – combines maximum visual effect with minimum greenhouse heating bills! His aim is to create 'magic and mystery and a touch of drama.'

And finally for the encouragement of all those who have just decided to 'do something' about an unsatisfactory garden, we have included one instant garden, belonging to designer Julian Treyer-Evans. All our other designers had gardens which had been established for some, if not always many, years – though with the passion of keen gardeners they were often finishing, renewing or entirely recreating some of the garden areas. Julian Treyer-Evans, notable for being probably the only garden designer who has designed a romantic garden with in-built jokes, had no garden to speak of when this book was first being planned. Although it is always unfair to put an absolutely newly made garden alongside established gardens, he nevertheless volunteered to make a garden from scratch.

In the four months while the other gardens were being photographed, he transformed a small back garden with a crazy paving path and a concrete rock garden up one side into an interesting three-level garden with borrowed landscape from the nearby playing field. Every paving stone, every brick and every square of turf was put into place with his own hands in the time left over from his own work. The result was proof not just that a professional designer can transform an unpromising garden, but also that the results can be enjoyed almost immediately. 'People won't wait for years to see results nowadays,' he says. 'They move houses quite often so they want to see results soon enough to enjoy them.'

In comparing the work of 12 such different garden designers, we can learn much – not just in the technical abilities of their work or even just the beauty of their overall designs. There is a lesson perhaps for the inner man. Gardeners, on the whole, seem to have developed not just their own craft but an assortment of human virtues such as kindness, hospitality, humour and tenderness. They are, more often than not, good people as well as good gardeners and the designers in this book give advice and encouragement.

In addition, there is one quality all had in common, despite the diversity of their approach. It is that underrated virtue, acceptance – demonstrated in choosing the plants to fit in with the soil and situation, often working within a small space, using and adapting to those gifts of nature like streams and lakes or nearby landscape. The beauty in our gardens comes from co-operation with, rather than forceful mastery of, nature. It was this thought, perhaps, that made Michael Balston say: 'A designer is just a link in the chain.'

Creating a garden allows us to dream a little. It is four hundred years since Francis Bacon wrote his essay on gardens. Yet his words invite us into a garden we still recognise, where there is perpetual spring, fine hedges, 'things of beauty in season' and 'the breath of flowers... far sweeter in the air, where it comes and goes like the warbling of music'. Garden designers are the professional friends who make possible the transformation of our dreams into reality.

● **John Brookes' garden archway** .

Restoring old gardens

During his working week John Sales keeps a designer's eye on fifty landscape parks, 110 gardens and various other cultivated areas, and twenty-six national plant collections. At weekends he cultivates his own rather smaller garden with its orchard, wildflower meadow and woodland walk.

As chief gardens adviser to the National Trust he is responsible for making and keeping all their gardens and parks attractive. Some 350 gardeners work for the Trust and with the help of three assistants each of the 110 gardens must be visited twice yearly.

Knot gardens, herb gardens, eighteenth-century landscape parks, Victorian bedding out schemes, and dotty eccentric gardens with a little bit of everything – all this wide variety of styles comes under his eye. He must maintain and preserve the gardens, and sometimes re-create them almost from scratch.

'I find it very creative,' he says. 'We do a lot of designing and planning on the ground – walking round with the head gardener suggesting how a garden could look even better.'

The yearly visits alone mean an enormous amount of travelling from the early spring garden of Trengwainton not far from Land's End to the vast rock garden and pinetum at Cragside not far from the Scottish border – and across the Irish sea to Mount Stewart, Lady Londonderry's great masterpiece of a garden in Northern Ireland.

● **(right) John Sales sits near the *Chrysanthemum frustescens* 'Vancouver Pink'. *Anchusa azurea* (below).**

Yet, despite this, John Sales manages to keep up a large garden of his own without any outside help, except for some (but not all) of the mowing and hedge cutting which is done by his wife, Lyn, or one or other of their three sons. Two-and-a-half acres of this is the garden proper. Somehow he manages to spend up to fifteen hours a week working at it. 'He will occasionally get up at 6.30 am to garden for a couple of hours before going into the office,' says his wife, Lyn. 'People catch gardening: there's no cure for it, and it's happened to him.' Luckily he lives only a few miles from the National Trust office in Cirencester, Gloucestershire.

Before joining the Trust many years ago he was a lecturer at an agricultural college. 'As I got higher up the ladder, I found I was getting further away from plants which are my real interest. So I joined the Trust as part of a radical reappraisal of my career, when I was in my late thirties.'

He took over the garden with its 1930s house in the early eighties. At the same time he bought a strip of woodland on one side, and a small strip of field on the other which he used to plant a small orchard, a small nuttery, and to make a small patch of wildflower meadow.

The garden (like many of his new National Trust properties) needed renewing. The surrounding beech hedges, and one derelict lawn had to

● Magenta *Geranium psilostemon* (left). In the garden's woodland white foxgloves and biennial sea holly have seeded themselves (right).

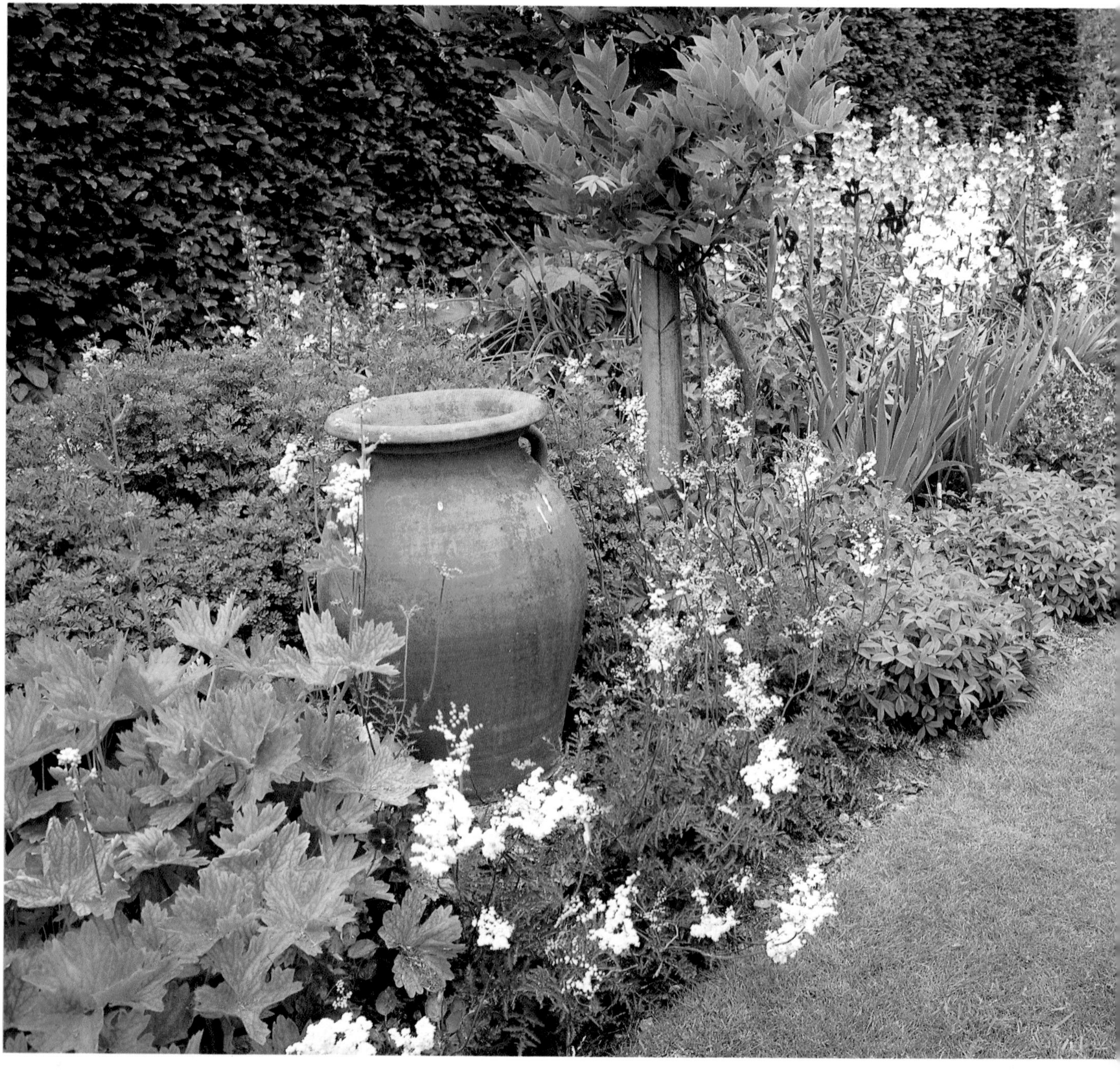

be cut and fed back into good condition. All round the rectangular lawn which was completely resewn he created large flower borders up to 20 feet wide in places.

'I like large borders. They give you good scope for big plants and for big drifts of one plant,' he says, ignoring the fact that such large borders are a design challenge that some gardeners cannot live up to.

On one side of the garden he has planted soft colours – pale blues, pinks and mauves. Opposite are hot colours like yellows, oranges and scarlets. At the top of the garden is a blue and white border of a 'mingled' design – his phrase for it.

This illustrates one of John Sales' most important aims, that of keeping a succession of colour and interest in the garden throughout the year. The border starts with blue and white grape hyacinths and chionodoxas, scillas, snowflakes and forget-me-nots, and continues through the summer with irises, blue and white campanulas and violas, Iceberg roses, Jacob's ladders, and blue agapanthus. Later on white Japanese anemones, blue Michaelmas daisies and white fuschias keep up the colour theme.

● **One of the borders is in deliberately 'mingled' shades of blues and whites (left). A drift of *Campanula latiloba* 'Alba' and 'Hidcote Amethyst' (below).**

'I'm not a plant collector. I don't feel I have to have one of everything. I just plant things I like that will do well where they are. I just like plants. I'm not a plant snob.' Yet almost every plant seems special. He has ancient pinks, with the real clove scent, like 'Bat's Double Red' and 'Brympton Red.' John Sales is not like the gardeners who point out some antique rarity, barely alive and miserably ill-looking. He grows plants that do well in the limey Cotswold soil.

He likes many different plants from day lilies and everlasting sweet peas to red hot pokers. 'It's unfashionable to like pokers, but I do. I've got quite a few different kinds – 'Little Maid', 'Wrexham Buttercup', 'Bressingham Torch', 'Green Jade', and, of course, 'Dawn'. Then there's 'Brimstone' and *galapinii* for later on.'

Growing one plant through another is a favourite trick of his. There is *Clematis flammula* growing through *Lonicera pileata*; *Clematis jouiniana* scrambling through shrubs; from an old apple tree there is *Clematis* 'Perle d'Azur' looking down at you, and through the yellow *Lonicera nitida* there is growing *Clematis durandii*.

● **Acers, yellow conifers and berberises (left), add their colour to the garden. Hostas and the perennial *Geranium* 'Johnson's Blue' (below).**

But it is the range of his own garden which is so impressive – lovely old roses, beautiful perennials, clematises, and naturalised lilies and alliums in the wood. At every point you pause there is an interesting plant growing in the most natural way. 'I'm just gardening to please myself. I try to keep my garden straightforward and simple,' he says. In this he has succeeded. For despite all the rare plants and unusual varieties of flowers, the most ignorant person in the world would enjoy the garden without recognising any of these. It has what is most important of all – the fragrance and beauty of an English country garden.

The National Trust gardens make up the most popular part of its many possessions and since John Sales joined their staff there has been a constant addition of two or three new gardens every year. Each new acquisition needs his careful attention.

The Trust has restored and redesigned several gardens since he joined. One of the first was Westbury Court Garden near Gloucester, a formal water garden with hedges and canals laid out at the end of the seventeenth century and the last of its kind remaining in England. While he was still assistant to the then chief gardens adviser, John Sales supervised Westbury Court's replanting. 'There were good records telling us precisely what they had bought and how they did it.

● **Chrysanthemum frutescens 'Vara', a yellow marguerite daisy (left), and (right) yellow *Corydalis lutea* and pink thrift in front of marguerite daisies in one of the many pots in the garden.**

We tried to follow these as closely as we could. It was a museum approach – as far as that's possible in gardening!'

Erdigg near Wrexham in Wales was rather different. An engraving in the house showed how the eighteenth-century formal garden had looked, and John Sales tried to restore the grand lines of this. 'But the last owner had been rather an eccentric recluse and in two-and-a-half centuries nothing in the house had been thrown away. So we left a kind of nineteenth- and twentieth-century overlay in the garden, a sort of dottiness that went with the place.'

Now his great challenge is Biddulph Grange Garden, near Stoke-on-Trent. A hospital was built in the garden in the 1930s but the garden, originally designed by James Bateman and Edward Cooke surprisingly survived

more or less intact. The National Trust has been raising funds to restore it. There are precise records here too, but the place itself has changed. Nearby buildings have created an ugly skyline and the original trees have grown very tall. 'Bateman put in twenty times more conifers than we would need to.'

Some Trust members would like every garden to be Sissinghurst. At Gawthorpe Hall, just outside Padiham in Lancashire, Sir Charles Barry had laid out a garden with a huge radiating parterre with bedding plants inside it. When the Trust took it over the parterre had been filled with mixed bush roses which John Sales describes as 'a feeble solution to something that demands bold treatment'. With only a few staff, they couldn't go back to the original labour-intensive Victorian bedding. So instead they filled the parterre with golden privet cut knee high edged with dwarf purple berberis. 'Everyone said it was vulgar! Perhaps so, but we think it was nearer the original than the roses.'

'We try to keep each garden unique. It's really important that there shouldn't be just one style of National Trust garden, so when there's no garden there, we would look at the history of the place and try to do something in keeping with it. If there's any touch of individuality, then we try to draw that out, if possible.'

● **Growing out of the gravel are clumps of *Iris* 'Mission Ridge' (left). One of the rare plants in John Sales' garden is the double red *Nasturtium* 'Hermione Gnashof' (right), which has to be overwintered in the greenhouse and grown from cuttings each spring.**

Designing gardens is not like designing other things. They cannot be made at a stroke. We are dealing with a process, not an object and all the designer can do is to set this process off in the right direction with the appropriate ingredients and taking into account the site, its opportunities and its limitations.

Gardens are made by the people who look after them; only they can ensure, as far as possible, that gardens become established and develop as they should. Rarely is it possible to be precise at the outset: who can say that they are not frequently surprised by the response of plants, at least in detail? Details are important in gardens, especially in intimate flower gardens, which depend for much of their effect on the sum of their important details.

Gardens are constantly being made and remade, quickly and accurately reflecting the quality and style of the upkeep and the character of the person in charge. With gardens that are meant to survive – longer that is than the term of a garden festival or beyond the photographs for a magazine – design, development and upkeep, even restoration, are all parts of the same process.

John Sales

Ten 'forgotten' gardens to visit

John Sales believes that many Trust gardens are still underappreciated. Here is his top ten list of undiscovered Trust gardens.

Acorn Bank, Temple Sowerby, near Penrith, Cumbria. A walled garden with lovely spring bulbs and a summer herb garden.

Castle Drogo, Drewsteignton, Devon. An Edwardian granite castle with formal rosebuds round a sunken lawn, and mixed herbaceous borders in the shape of an Indian motif.

Dunham Massey, near Altrincham, Cheshire. A grand garden with an orangery, deer house and statues. The moat, parkland walks, and flower borders have all been restored, with a bog garden, rhododendrons and other flowering shrubs.

Emmetts, Ide Hill, Sevenoaks, Kent – a hillside arboretum of trees and shrubs laid out at the turn of the century by William Robinson. Lovely in bluebell time. It was badly damaged by the 1987 hurricane but is still beautiful.

Lyte Cary Manor, Somerton, Somerset. A series of garden rooms with green corridors between them – shrubs, herbaceous plants and a sunken rose garden.

● **The terraces and borders in the well-garden at Acorn Bank (above); purple wisteria frames stone steps in the Castle Drogo gardens (below, left); and the yellow and blue border in bloom at Wallington (below, right).**

Moseley Old Hall, Wolverhampton, West Midlands. This is where Charles II took refuge on the run from Cromwell's troops. To commemorate this the gardens are seventeenth century – including a knot garden with coloured gravel and no plant later than 1651!

Peckover House, North Brink, Wisbech, Cambridgeshire. A small Victorian garden with many exotic plants and flowers and even oranges ripening in the conservatory. A garden for every season of the year.

Powis Castle, Welshpool, Powys, Wales. A terraced garden in the Italian style with a glorious array of flowers. Yew hedges and statues make this formal in style but a wilderness opposite the terraces has informal winding paths through trees, magnolias and rhododendrons.

Rowallane Gardens, Saintfield, Ballynahinch, Co. Down, Northern Ireland. Summer flowering trees, shrubs and herbaceous plants with fuschias and shrubbery in the walled garden. In the rock garden primulas, heathers, and dwarf shrubs have interest throughout the year.

Wallington Hall, Cambo, Morpeth, Northumberland. An eighteenth-century park and garden with trees, a grotto and ponds. There is a walled garden with fragrant roses, honeysuckles and shrubs and a viewing platform from which you see a flower-edged stream winding into the shrubbery.

● **Agapanthus and anemones in the summer flower border at Peckover House.**

Creating a romantic garden

Mark Rumary believes gardens should be pretty. Unashamedly pretty like his own small garden full of flowers. 'I like giving my gardens the Laura Ashley look,' he says, half joking.

The Laura Ashley look, or rather the Mark Rumary look, is what so many

● **The Moorish garden's straight paths broken by floppy flowers (below). Mark with Bruno the English Setter (right).**

gardeners dream about – a combination of flowers and colour and scent to delight the eye and charm the senses. His gardens create this romantic effect. In the world of designer jeans and designer frocks, the mark of his gardens is that they are not designer anything.

To modern design fashionables it is all very shocking. One-upmanship in

the garden means preferring greens to pinks, prizing foliage above flowers, and heaven forbid that a garden should be pretty. Startling, remarkable, even dramatic, but not pretty. Prettiness, say the designer snobs, is out.

'One of those kind of designers came to look at my garden one day in late summer when because of some difficult weather nothing was out. I was terribly disappointed at the way it looked, but he said, 'Oh it's just green. What a wonderful garden.'

Yet that wasn't what I was aiming for at all.'

In summer the masses of pink, white and mauve scented flowers that fill his own garden in the small village of Yoxford in Suffolk are what most people want in their own gardens. Old roses, with their tightly packed flat blooms and romantic names, frame a garden full of old fashioned flowers like sweet rocket, columbines and five different kinds of Hattie's pin-cushions (known to the unromantic as astrantia).

'Most Englishwomen want a flower garden,' he says. 'When I design gardens I don't feel pressured into doing something else. After all look at the really popular gardens like Hidcote and Sissinghurst. People love them because they have bags of romantic colour and scent.'

● **Mark Rumary has created charming vistas in all directions, using focal points like this sundial (left) to catch the eye. The secluded English country garden look with lawn stretching down to the patio with afternoon tea (below).**

He has been designing gardens for Notcutts for many years, the nursery firm in Suffolk who have managed to combine old-fashioned standards with modern techniques. The Notcutts clientele in East Anglia are traditionally English – often titled, old money rather than new, and not too worried by the ups and downs of the Stock Exchange since they invest, rather than gamble, their wealth. Occasionally, however, he flies off to the Middle East to design a palace garden there!

Yuppies who want a dazzling display of brickwork and architectural plants, or social climbers who want grandeur in the garden wouldn't go to Mark Rumary in the first place. His clients just want good taste gardens – well constructed terraces, walls, lawns and nice flowers with the sound of bees and the scent of old roses and flowering shrubs.

'I'm fond of soft colours. I think they are beautiful and they are also easier to use in country gardens than the bright hard ones.' Though his own garden has a orange and red border at one end, the predominant colours are dreamy pinks and whites.

Mark Rumary is discretion itself. He would think it bad form and bad manners to reveal the names of his clients. His gardens in the stately homes of East Anglia are sometimes open to the public but he will not tell you which they are. Most of them look as if they have been there for

● **Mark Rumary prunes back the wisteria which he grows as an unusual standard. Behind him to the left are greenish yellow euphorbias and to the right pink allium flowerheads.**

generations. He has won so many gold medals at Chelsea for Notcutts that a year without one is an exception.

In the 1970s, at the end of the Callaghan era when it looked as if Britain was the sick man of Europe, Mark Rumary's confidence faltered, Notcutts were worried whether private garden work would continue, and he and the firm started looking for work in landscaping factories and housing developments. They discovered a cut-throat market with abysmal standards. 'The workforce were used to doing quality work.

They couldn't do it that badly,' he recalls. 'Now we only do that kind of work if it is of a certain standard. But we were wrong to think the private work was going to disappear. Individuals kept coming to us. Apart from anything else we can do the lot from Notcutts. There's no subcontracting with different firms. We can design, build and plant you a garden from start to finish.'

I always know I have succeeded when I hear the owner say they did the designing themselves. It means I have done what they really wanted

though perhaps they didn't know how to do it themselves.'

When he moved into his own garden it was a sea of ground elder and other weeds. Though it is only about a third of an acre, he turned it into various different areas by planting hedges. An old stableyard became a shaded white and green garden: the vegetable patch was turned into a kind of Moorish garden with a raised pond and fountain.

● **Mark and Bruno at the raised pond. Behind is the topiary arch leading to the lawn.**

Though the dizzy abundance of flowers looks completely informal, they conceal very firm design lines. The Moorish garden has absolutely straight paths leading up to the pond softened by the old roses and cottage flowers that flop over the paving. Topiary arches, pots full of white pansies, and a couple of little box topiary specimens make focal points.

It is a highly romantic garden – decorated by the white doves that flutter down on to the lawn from the stable dovecote and by the elegant figure of Bruno, the English setter. The dog's soft blue and white ringlets merge beautifully into the pinks and mauves of the flowers. A robin and a thrush nest in the greenhouse.

'I use soft colours rather than hard ones, and I use colours out of a narrowish range. To stop it looking boring, you repeat the same colour in differently shaped flowers. There's no harm in wandering round with a flower to try and see where it will look best.' Spiky grey artichoke foliage forms a background for pink sweet rocket. Old roses pick up the pinks and whites in their floppy arching shapes. Then pink allium flowerheads repeat the colour.

The lawn is weed-free, deep green and totally manicured. Each plant looks well and the informality of the flowers conceals a plantsman's taste for unusual specimens. With characteristic modesty, Mark Rumary will say 'I have made many mistakes in choosing plants. It is his modesty which conceals the skill behind such a beautiful creation. Indeed his garden reveals the essence of traditional English character – a gardener's perfectionism which lets flower a highly emotional and romantic beauty.

● **The white and green garden with hostas and urn (left), and (below) elegant Bruno matches the garden's colour schemes.**

Getting the skeleton of the garden right is the thing to concentrate on, when starting a new garden. 'It's too expensive to have to rip up paths and paving is just too expensive.' Spend time thinking about what you want the garden for – places to sit in, where the paths should run, where the compost heap, washing line and bonfire should be placed. Draw out a plan and try to think what the view will be from the house.

'Spend your money on good paving, a well laid and decent trellis. Plants can wait. You can build up these from cuttings and bits from friends. But the permanent things like paving, hedges, and trees are where you should spend your money initially.'

'Start with a firm framework, then you can mess about with plants as softeners,' he says. Strong regular design lines disappear under waves of plants. His own pink, white and grey garden with the raised pond, illustrates this.

It is the gardener's dream to pave with real York stone – but few can afford it. 'Some of the mock York stones in concrete look quite good, unlike earlier products.' He uses Marshall's York stone heritage paving, but warns: 'If you are going to use these, then make sure you use them whole. They cut badly and the cut edges expose the concrete aggregate.' When he wants to grow plants between the paving instead of knocking off the corners, he leaves a one to two-inch gap between slabs.

He also uses a paving bricks, granite sets and a new kind of set manu-factured by Blanc de Bierges. 'Use brick and sets when you want a small unit. Brick is good for curving paths and the sets are useful for circles.' In a big area, he will use a mixture of paving making a pattern 'like a carpet. It puts some variation into it. Otherwise a large paved area can look dull.'

Crazy paving he rarely uses. 'I would never use it with a modern house, but just occasionally it might go with a period house of the 1920s and 1930s. I set it within brick or within York stone as a definite feature. I hate tiny bits of crazy paving with white edging. But large pieces with even joints can look all right. But I'd never recommend it for amateurs – it looks more crazy than paving!'

Gardeners should also remember what Mark Rumary calls 'service paths'. These are small paths running along-side all hedges and often at the back of flower borders too. 'It means you can get near to the hedge to clip it, and can weed the back of the border without standing on the flowers.'

To make the garden boundaries, try hedges. These are far cheaper than walls, and often look more beautiful. Mark Rumary's Moorish garden is cut off from the main lawn with a beech hedge cut into two arches over the entrance paths. The effect is wonderful. 'It's not just that hedges are cheaper: they look better too. Lots of my wealthy clients who don't have to worry about money, choose hedges just for that reason. They look lovely in country gardens.'

● **Self-seeded _Allium christophii_ next to the rare _salvia interrupta_.**

For me there are three essentials in the making of a good garden. First, there must be a well-conceived plan which is expertly implemented, for beneath the flowers there must be good 'bones'. Secondly, I would hope to find horticultural interest combined with good maintenance. Thirdly, and this is the most difficult to achieve, a well defined character.

The initial design must take into account the site, the character of the house, and not only the tastes of the owners but their needs. As well as giving visual pleasure each part must 'work', for designing is essentially a practical business. When it comes to the structure I like well built terraces paths, pools and pergolas which can be a foil or support for plants.

Horticultural interest does not depend on using rare plants, but in choosing those which are right for the design and colour schemes, the soil and the climate.

The degree of maintenance must be in accordance with the character of the design. Without attention a wild garden will soon get out of hand, whilst too much tidiness can create a sterile effect, even in a formal garden.

When all these essentials are in harmony then a garden of character will result; one which will appeal to our intellect, senses and, hopefully, emotions.

Mark Rumary

Conserving and using rare plants

The plight of forgotten flowers, threatened with extinction if they fall out of fashion, concerns Iris Strachan. She is a Scottish garden designer turned conservationist, dedicated to rescuing some of the plants of the past before they die out. In her Peeblesshire garden, about 800 feet up surrounded by hills, she keeps the national collection of some twenty different comfrey plants – flowers with modest blooms but rampant growth, that needed a home in 1986.

'My enthusiasm for comfreys started when I found a patch of the white kind in a garden I was redesigning. I pinched a bit and it was the beginning of my collection.'

Her career as a garden designer started in the sixties when her four children were growing up and she was looking for something more to do. She started helping out a famous Scottish designer, Kate Hawkins, then took a two-year part-time landscaping course. Since then she has designed some fifty-four gardens – from small Edinburgh town gardens to large country gardens including a couple of overseas gardens in Luxembourg and Corfu. But as most of her clients are from the east coast of Scotland, she often has to design with the cold and wet and wind in mind.

Where soft southern designers can go to town with pretty delicate flowers, she has to think of plants that will survive in adverse conditions. Her own country garden, near Broughton in the highest county in Britain,

couldn't be a better testing ground. 'We can have frost every single month, including the occasional August frost. And we can have snow as late as June, though it doesn't lie if it falls then,' she explains. 'A lot of my planting here is simply trees for shelter. Things that could grow down south can't overwinter here. I have to take my rosemary and my bay into the house during the winter.'

There are hundreds of trees in all, including a collection of different rowans, birches and many different willows near the burn that runs through the garden down the valley. Her husband Michael, retired from shipping and now trustee for the

National Library of Scotland, has planted many of these.

As a further precaution against the wind, the garden is split into smaller gardens with thick shrubs or hedges in between. One of the hedges, framing her yellow border, is made up of huge strong redcurrant bushes, which were there in the garden when they took it over.

Hers is what she calls 'a garden of thugs' – plants that would be horribly rampant and invasive in the south are strong enough to survive the

● **High winds make Iris Strachan's country garden an ordeal for all plants (below). Hills provide a beautiful borrowed landscape (right).**

Peeblesshire cold and its gale force 9 winds. 'Living in the coldest spot in Scotland, as I do, has been a great help in designing Scottish gardens.'

The thugs in her garden include oriental poppies from dark red to palest pink, the wild blue meadow cranesbill and its relative the spreading *Geranium wlassovianum*, Welsh poppies, tall grey mulleins, alstromerias, the variegated grass known as gardener's garters, and lady's mantle otherwise known as *Alchemilla mollis*. These plants, which might be rampaging pests in a southern garden, survive sedately in her borders or are planted in the grass to grow wild through its stems.

Her shrubs have to be equally hardy. She has lots of different elders – yellow-leaved, variegated, and purple leaved – rugosa shrub roses, and wild sweet briars, the roses known to poets as 'sweet eglantines' with their apple-scented leaves and wild rose pink flowers.

● **Iris near the yellow border (left). Yellow-leaved elder (top), and meadow cranesbill growing out of long grass (below).**

Hybrid tea roses (which she grows in her Edinburgh town garden) wouldn't stand a chance in Peeblesshire. Instead she grows Scotch roses, the spiny shrub roses that were popular 200 years ago before the advent of repeat flowering roses. There are eight of these in her garden, including a double yellow one and an even rarer double purple.

While southern gardens have to contend with greenfly, mildew and black spot, her pests are larger – voles, rabbits, hares and deer. Given a chance, the deer will eat out the leading shoots of trees and browse shrubs down to the ground.

There is not a single heather plant in her garden. 'I would never design a heather garden, not for a million pounds. I don't think they are anything to do with country gardens and

● The *rus in urbe* look with wild strawberries and roses in the Edinburgh front garden (below and right).

I don't like the sort of suburban style that they represent. I try to design gardens that give an impression of countryside within the town,' she says. 'Most of my clients say they want something like Sissinghurst but I tell them they can't have that in Scotland.'

There are consolations in the fierce climate. 'You can grow wonderful gentians here. When my daughter married we had enough of them to make posies for five bridesmaids.'

Here design style is based on a fairly traditional plan. 'I have no wiggles, no island beds. I like decent walkways which are broad enough, and good steps. I never put the proper herbaceous borders just full of perennial flowers. I use shrubs and herbaceous flowers together, and I group colours – though I do like the occasional spiffing clash!'

Even high up in the Peeblesshire hills, there are rarities in her garden. She has a naturalised clump of the melancholy thistle, a wild thistle without thorns so rare that it is now protected by law, and some of the Scotch roses are far from common.

Other rare plants she keeps in her Edinburgh town garden, which is protected against wind and cold. There she has a gravelled back garden with a raised bed of shrub roses and herbaceous plants, and in the front hybrid tea roses underplanted with masses of red and white alpine strawberries.

● **A pink among the Edinburgh strawberries (left), and the rare *Cirsium heterophyllum*, in the country garden (right).**

As one of the first Scots to see the need for plant conservation, Iris Strachan is committed to helping rescue the old varieties. She was one of the first members of the National Council for the Conservation of Plants and Gardens and heads the local group. So rare plants often rest for a few days or weeks in her Edinburgh garden on their way to exhibitions or flower shows. Even so, she is strictly practical in her approach to designing others' gardens. 'I'd always rather use a common plant of the right colour than a rare plant that doesn't match, or that just won't grow.'

You don't have to be an expert gardener or botanist to help rescue rare plants. The National Council for the Conservation of Plants and Gardens (NCCPG) welcomes all members, including enthusiasts who know little or nothing. 'We have a great need for helpers. Everybody wants to do the glamorous things like keeping a national collection, but most of all we need people who will help man exhibitions and generally be Indians instead of chiefs.'

Plant sales not only help raise funds but are a way of spreading rare plants to a larger number of gardeners. Members can help grow on and propagate some of the rare plants for these sales.

So far there are about 400 so called national reference collections of plants in Britain but there are hundreds of

● **Iris Strachan is fond of everlasting sweet peas, delicate flowers neglected by many gardeners (left). Her Edinburgh back garden (far right).**

cultivated plants threatened with extinction. The idea of the collections is that each represents all or most of the varieties of a particular plant – like a kind of living reference section of a library.

The twenty different comfreys in Iris Strachan's garden represent all the different varieties – wild and cultivated – known in Britain. There are blue, pink and red flowered comfreys, and various kinds with variegated leaves. Some are different species: others just different gardening varieties.

In keeping the collection Iris Strachan has to keep detailed notes of each variety – the size, the way it grows, the details of its flowers. She must make sure that she has more than just one plant, so that if one dies she can replace it. 'Luckily I've got buckets of room in Peeblesshire. I couldn't have such a rampant plant in my town garden.'

The comfrey collection is a small one but some species have literally hundreds of different cultivated varieties – for instance, the heather collection sponsored by Bells Whisky will eventually have more than a thousand different kinds of heathers.

All gardeners can do their bit to help keep the rarer varieties going by making sure they buy their plants from good nurseries which offer a wide variety of plants, rather than the garden centres which only carry common stock. Nurseries run by people who care for plants should be encouraged.

'If you are interested in helping rescue rare plants, the first thing to do is to join the NCCPG, says Iris Strachan. 'Then if you do get a rare plant, don't keep it to yourself. Always give bits of it away to others to make sure that if you lose yours, there will still be some in existence.'

Propagate perennials by splitting big plants into several smaller ones. Take cuttings from shrubs. If the plant is an annual or a biennial, let the seedheads form and collect the seed. Distribute this round the good gardeners that you know. Generosity to others helps conserve rare plants.

Out there in the garden are all the components of life. Chaos to be controlled, wind and storm to be endured, perfection of form and colour to be appreciated, death and decay, predators, but also an individual Eden.

For a client my purpose is to relate their aspirations to the opportunities and limitations of the site. Once the hard surfaces – terrace, paths etc. – and decent trees are there, for that is basically all you need to make a garden, then the more personal pleasures of shrubs and herbaceous plants and their arrangements can develop.

For myself, in my garden I prefer a sweet disorder to over-organisation; the good pleasures of planting, the feel of the earth, colour, scent, texture and form of each individual plant.

I did not start my garden diary until 1981 – previous spasmodic efforts were never sustained. It is an enormous help to know the exact date of sowing or planting, the origin of the plant, successes, failures, presents from friends, fun and parties. To record these things and to maximise your hard battle to make a garden, you should start your garden diary the day you start to plan your plot. It is a book which you will never find dull. From my diary I am compiling a catalogue of plants for a cold climate which I hope will be of use to other labourers on high and windy sites.

Iris Strachan.

Tropical jungles

Some designers give the room outside look to the garden: others bring the wildlife look to it. Myles Challis goes much much further. He lets in the jungle. You step into a tropical rain forest when you walk into his small back yard behind a Victorian terraced house in Leytonstone, East London. Huge jungle looking plants have to be brushed aside as you walk down a winding path to a forest pool.

He's been called a 'leaf fanatic' and he's a self-confessed flower snob who likes esoteric varieties with 'non-gaudy' flowers. Not for him the hard landscaping of the yuppie garden with its patio for parties, paving for low maintenance and raised beds for easy weeding. Nor does the country garden look with herbaceous borders and 'nice' lawns appeal to him.

His gardens are unashamedly exotic. Instead of looking down on to grass and flowers, you look up towards gigantic tropical leaves. The visitor to his garden walks along the forest floor in relative humidity while huge exotic tropical leaves tower above. Only they are not tropical at all. They just look that way. This is the secret of a Myles Challis rain forest garden. It might look like the South American jungle. It might even smell like one. But it's not. It grows in the ordinary cold climate of Britain.

'It all started when I was taken to Kew to the Aroid house which was very jungly. I can remember walking down the path pushing aside the huge leaves. It started something for me.'

When he went home he took over the long greenhouse at the back of their Hampstead house and when his 14th birthday arrived asked his father if he could have heating installed in it. Within a few years he had filled it with an amazing collection largely of aroids, which he had gathered from collectors and nurserymen.

Lush climbers, philodendrons and scindapsus, covered mossy columns and tree trunks along with orchids, and pitcher plants (nepenthes). On the ground under shade of heliconias flourished the beautifully marked and patterned leaves of calatheas, anthuriums, and alocasias. 'It went on until the oil crisis made it impossible. I panicked. I went to the library to see what I could do. It was then I realised there were a lot of exotic looking plants you could grow outside without artificial heating. That's when I discovered the outdoor exotics and changed course from indoor to outdoor gardening.'

He took up garden designing in the early eighties and made his first impact as one of the youngest designers at Chelsea Flower show with his Neptune's garden in 1986. It won a silver medal: it was too odd for a gold. But it was noticed.

He moved into his own garden at about the same time, got rid of the only growing thing there, a gnarled old apple tree and eschewed the temptation of a town patio in favour of

● **Myles Challis in his jungle.**

jungle. 'If I had more space here I would have a patio, but space is too precious. Luckily the jungly garden adapts itself well to his small narrow space, only 20ft by 40ft. His hardy palm, which has survived two winters, grows upwards not outwards. The three different bamboo clumps are vertical rather than horizontal in their growth.

'One of my beliefs is that you should never be able to take in any garden in just one glance. You should walk down it and have surprises as you go.' His own garden certainly follows this philosophy. The curving path leads down to a pool – not only do you not see the pool till you are nearly falling into it, but on the way down new plants reveal themselves when you brush aside other plants in order to see where you are going.

'I feel the look of an informal garden is much more aesthetically pleasing. it's much more unwinding. Most people have terrific stress in their jobs now: they need more than ever to relax and unwind. People who are in stressful office jobs are in the indoor jungle. I have created what you might call the jungle outdoors.'

The jungle garden has some very obvious benefits. 'The competition is just too much for weeds. They can't grow. Anything less than about a foot or 18 inches can't make it,' he says with satisfaction

About a quarter of the plants in his garden are sub-tropical, and need wintering in a greenhouse. There are

● **Eye level green geometry — stems contrasting with horizontal foliage (left and right).**

● **Yellow ligularia flowerspikes glow out among the green bamboos and palms.**

red flowered cannas, white arum lilies, angel trumpet daturas, gingers and an Abyssinian banana tree – all of them in large pots. 'These extend the season. In the average English garden, things start looking tatty by August. But these tender exotics are looking their best when the ordinary herbaceous plants are dishevelled.'

His style of planting makes even the more familiar plants look exotic. Ligularias and rodgerias take on a tropical aspect, while the huge gunnera near the pond and even the Himalayan cowslips become unfamiliar – partly because his rain forest pool is just that. There are no stone edges, not even a pebbly beach, just forest earth leading down to water.

Plants like the pink pokeweed and *Crambe cordifolia* (a gigantic kale with a huge stem of massed tiny white flowers) are used by adventurous gardeners in herbaceous borders. Here, surrounded by the Indian horse chestnut tree or a potted tree fern you notice their strangeness. Even the hydrangea (*Hydrangea sargentiana* not the common *macrophylle)* looks exotic. Furry kiwi fruit vines take the place of honeysuckle or rambling roses.

You can get the exotic look for your garden, without needing a greenhouse at all, by following Myles Challis' suggestions for plants, which simply requires choosing plants with 'tropical forest' leaves.

For hedging choose Portuguese laurel *(Prunus lusitanica),* with its evergreen leaves and white flowerspikes in summer. 'Don't clip it into a hedge shape. Let it grow naturally. Just occasionally trim it back and always use secateurs not shears for a natural look.'

Bamboo is another hedging possibility, if you live in the west of England where winters will not be too hard. The most common bamboo is *Arundinaria japonica,* but it flowered and died off in 1986 so stocks are low. Myles' preference is for either *Arundinaria murieliae* or *nitida* – the latter needs some protection from strong winds. 'Bamboo is good in small gardens for hiding things like compost heaps or for diverting a path around. They look nice in almost any kind of garden, but particularly an exotic one!'

For specimen trees, try a hardy palm or the Indian horse chestnut instead of the boring flowering cherry. For a small garden *Acer negundo* 'Flamingo' with serrated leaves which start pink and turn variegated, looks quite exotic, grown either as a shrub or a small tree. Another possibility is a *Paulownia tomentosa,* pollarded down to the ground each winter, and allowing just one shoot to develop through the summer.

For shrubs there is the familiar *Fatsia japonica.* 'You see them in old Tarzan films, where they are used to create a jungle look. They need shade not sun, so they usually look ill in English gardens.' Camellias, *Hydrangea aspera* or *sargentiana,* purplish pittosporum, and *Eucalyptus globulus* all make handsome tropical-looking shrubs.

From the herbaceous border, he has borrowed ligularias and rodgersias, both plants with wide palmate leaves. The huge *Ligularia wilsoniana* has eight-feet high flowers with good seedheads. Hostas, particularly the large blue *Hosta sieboldiana* 'Elegans', phormiums, and pink pokeweed *(Phytolacca clavigera)* with its exotic pink spikes followed by black berries are other tropical-looking plants which are good growers.

The final touch to a Myles Challis garden would be to grow some annuals on the windowsill. 'If you planted some castor oil plants on the windowsill in February or March, you could plant them out in late May or June and you would have fine plants by August. 'Another possibility is the huge *Nicotiana sylvestris,* which has large white fragrant blooms up to six feet high.

'These aren't particularly difficult plants.' he says reassuringly. 'All the plants I suggest flourish. I don't consider a plant worthy of cultivation unless it makes vigorous growth. These plants look tropical but they are *happy* growing outside.'

Myles Challis's garden is not like any other though it might remind the visitor of one of the British sub-tropical gardens like Tresco or Inverewe, or a wilder version of one of the botanic garden greenhouses. Asked to sum it up, the man who brought the jungle to E1 simply says: 'Magic and mystery and a touch of drama – these are the most valuable things in any garden.'

● Red *Canna* 'Firebird', overwintered in the greenhouse, is put out in summer to give colour to the garden (above). The round leaves of yellow ligularia look surprisingly exotic in the Myles Challis' designer jungle (right).

To be a really good designer one has to have a combination of skills. One has of course to be a good plantsperson, one has to be a good draughtsperson with most importantly a good eye for perspective, and be artistic by nature. But I believe above all one has to be a visionary (preferably with a photographic mind) so that one can look at a site or garden and picture it as it could be regardless of how it looks at present.

My two most fervent beliefs are first, that an informal garden is better because it lends itself more readily to a relaxing atmosphere – it should be a place to escape the rigours of life. Secondly, it should always have water. Nothing adds so much life, interest and beauty to a garden as water.

When starting a garden from scratch, think of it as a stage set and begin by creating the backcloth. Establish first of all your boundaries, preferably using hedging with as many evergreens as possible, to hide from view your surroundings, especially buildings. You will than have an oasis and your stage is set for whatever you wish.

Myles Challis

Planning a formal garden

For a grandly formal garden, there is only one designer – Arabella Lennox-Boyd. She is one of Britain's most successful garden designers as well as one of the most fashionable. The Belgian Royal family asked her to design the gardens for the Palais du Belvedere, the residence of the heir to the throne, Prince Albert – the Belgian equivalent to Kensington Palace. She has done gardens for the top families of Europe and some of the most stylish gardens in Britain are hers.

Her own garden in the Lancashire constituency of her husband, Mark Lennox-Boyd, parliamentary private secretary to Mrs Thatcher, is a tribute to her designer eye. A love of beautiful plants, seen in the old roses and the magnolias growing out of long grass, has transformed a gloomy northern mansion.

She is not afraid of formality. 'The English are frightened of formality in a garden. The traditional English gardener will put a wavy path in the garden which can often look untidy. People who don't understand about plants are frightened of hard lines. Yet a straight path will look just as informal if you plant either side of it properly. If you use geometry when designing a garden, then you have balance. I feel lost in a garden which is not planned geometrically.'

Born in Rome, she spent her teenage years at an English girls' boarding school. 'I have not been consciously influenced by Italian gardens, but that sort of style seemed to come naturally to me. Perhaps the Renaissance architecture of Rome has unconsciously influenced me.'

It was while she was studying landscape architecture at the Thames Polytechnic that she started designing gardens in Britain and some abroad. When the Belgian Royal family asked her to redesign the Palais du Belvedere only two years after she had started, she gained a reputation for rather large grand gardens – though she does small town gardens as well as large country ones. 'If I am to do a really good garden for a client, the owner has to be interested in plants and love them or there has to be a head gardener who knows what he's doing.'

Nowadays she has an office in London with four employees and designs both English and, sometimes, European gardens. Combining this with two children (one daughter is grown-up) and the constituency duties expected of any MP's wife means a lot of hard work.

She has turned her own northern garden into something that looks like a light-drenched Tuscany villa. When she arrived a few years ago the Victorian house stood gloomily under a hillside of rhododendrons. More rhododendrons and laurels crowded round a long lake and an even longer lawn. 'I didn't understand it at all. It was all very dark and dank'. Now the

● **Looking across the feathery astilbes towards the Victorian house, which has a redesigned lake and new terraces.**

house has been resettled into the landscape by building new terraces which cascade with old roses. Little stone stairways lead to octagonal patches of grass, and a gazebo has been built over the stream. Eventually it will be covered with honeysuckle and roses.

The long dank stretch of water is now not so much a lake as a *pièce d'eau*, that frivolous French phrase which describes water in the garden. To conceal the outflow to the river there is a little waterside arbour – and because this is an Arabella Lennox-Boyd garden, an exactly matching twin has been built to balance, on the other side of the lake.

Everywhere the gloomy rhododendrons and laurels have been rooted out in favour of proper flowerbeds filled with shrubs, roses and little garden auriculas and primulas. If there are rhododendrons, they are there in their own right as flowering shrubs in a border, not just woodland cover.

Everywhere there is topiary in the making – a yew hedge to close in the top view of the garden, yews which will grow into balustrades near the end of the bridge, a yew stump being trained into a lion shape, upright Irish yews which will grow into natural columns. From the top terrace you can look down at little box edged beds with box balls at each corner.

● **The view from the bridge across the river with its charming gazebo (left). Looking down from the terrace to the little octagonal lawn and the lakeside (above, right). Sweet smelling old shrub roses and herbaceous plants clothe the terraces (right).**

The effect may be formal, but it is also frivolous like a Fragonard painting, thanks to lavish planting of flowering scented roses and shrubs. The sweet peas which grow in masses up bushy sticks out of a formal Versailles tubs sum up the combination.

'I think this climate needs a bit of jollity,' Arabella Lennox-Boyd says. 'I always say to my client that a garden's got to be fun. You should be able to go out and pick enormous bowls of sweet peas from the garden. If you are going to splash out on your garden, you should be able to fill up bowls and bowls of flowers, pick baskets of raspberries and baskets of *fraises du bois*. There should be a whole bed of Rembrandt tulips to pick in spring. I really enjoy mine.'

Her husband's contribution to the garden has been an obelisk sundial, designed with the help of a computer. 'I didn't invent it, but it's never been done quite like this before,' says Mark Lennox-Boyd. 'Unlike most sundials, this will tell the *right* time every day.'

When Arabella Lennox-Boyd is planning other people's gardens, she spends the first part of her time taking an enormously detailed survey of what is there already – the soil type, where the light falls, the wind, the shape of the ground, existing trees and walls. All this is written down rather

like the surveyor's report on a house. Then on paper with a compass, she will plan a new garden. Her hourly fee is expensive and some of the gardens she designs have sometimes cost six-figure sums to put into execution if her clients want lakes and terraces.

'I can also work on a cheaper level. I try to adjust to what the clients want me to do – as long as the client is really interested and I'm sure that the end result is going to satisfy me. The cost of a garden is the same as the cost of a house – so many square metres of garden will cost the same as so many square metres of house. To dig proper flowerbeds costs the same as having curtains made.'

'Don't be afraid of formality,' she advises. Even a small garden, or the traditional semi-detached long rectangular garden can look wonderful

● **The terraces leading down to the lakeside with its two lion statues (left). Sweet peas grown in a Versailles box sum up the garden's romantic style (above). Acers for foliage and Himalayan cowslips (right).**

using a formal design. Using her system, start your planning by taking a careful note on paper of what the garden is like now – where there is light or shade, if the soil is damp or dry, whether soil is acid or alkaline, the prevailing wind, existing mature trees, hedges and so forth. 'Start by being practical and remembering where you want the compost heap, the dustbins and so forth,' she says. 'If you have a long rectangular garden, divide it up into different sections.'

'Formality doesn't have to be all straight lines. You can use circles or semi-circles very effectively. Only make your curves balanced and regular. For instance if you have two very long borders, you could break

● **Arabella Lennox-Boyd on the bridge (left). A stone lion with a huge Scotch thistle (below), and hostas near the lake (right).**

them up using scollops down the side – repeating exactly the same shapes either side, rather than putting in ir-regular wavy lines. Get some graph paper, and do the plan on it using ruler and compass. Think about opening up a view, if there is a nice one, or closing it up to hide it or put the emphasis on something nearer. Look at books about design to get some ideas.'

● The symmetry of the paved terraces is broken up by old shrub roses and herbaceous plants which clothe them with colour and scent (above). *Eryngium giganteum*, nicknamed Miss Willmott's ghost after a famous gardener, seeds itself in the terrace (left). A little wooden bridge leads to an island in the lake (right).

Building new walls is very expensive but topiary can fulfil the same function much more cheaply. Putting in a yew hedge can give a structure to the garden and will not cost too much if you are prepared to wait for the yew to grow. 'It's a modern form of sculpture, but it needn't be elaborate. You can use balls or square shapes. Neither is it very hard work: herbaceous plants need more maintenance than a clipped hedge.'

Her approach is emotional as well as professional. 'Clients have feelings which you must always remember,' she says. 'Also when I go into a garden for the first time, I get a feeling about what it should be like. I try to remember this first impression, because it is almost always right.'

Her Fragonard or Versailles gardens will never come within the financial grasp of ordinary part-time gardeners, but her principles of formal design and frivolous planting are within the reach of us all. As she says: 'As I continue designing, I think more and more I look for balance, rhythm and focus in a garden. After all the herbaceous plants can disappear so quickly from a garden, but a good overall structure can last for generations.'

My childhood years were spent in rural Italy, cultivating a deep love of sun-drenched landscapes and the abundance of wild flowers. Italian villas, and frequent trips to Rome, instilled in me a great passion for the classical form. These early impressions remain vivid in my mind whenever I design, and are a fundamental part of my approach to design.

I confess to having a deep interest and instinct for plants, and feel that they should be planted in profusion to create a sensual effect as well as saving the busy gardener much time in weeding. A tip for anyone starting out with designing their garden is to picture the site in black and white in order to get an idea of the type of structure that you would like the garden to have. Once you have the desired form, you can then select plants to juxtapose interesting contrasts in shapes, sizes, and textures.

Although I feel it is most vital to read books on gardening, there is nothing more valuable than to visit gardens and to converse with gardeners – in this way one can get the feel as well as confidence of creating an original structure and style of planting.

My approach to designing a garden is to relate each garden to the house, and to the people who live in it. Gardens can look beautiful without being too expensive to create. The preparation of flower beds is very important – if you spend £1 on a plant then you should spend £3 on preparing the bed. Buttresses and box shapes of clipped yew hedging can be used to give structure to the shape of your garden. I feel that gardens should reflect the character of the owner by ascertaining one's own individual style. One should not be frightened to experiment with ideas. When the required look has been obtained, the garden will provide many years of pleasure and self satisfaction.

Ascott House, near Leighton Buzzard, a National Trust garden, is a fine example of a design in the Victorian grand and formal style. As a designer, I found this garden great fun to design as I was able to incorporate all types of architectural structures within the formal layout whilst keeping to the Victorian ornate style.

Arabella Lennox-Boyd

● **The view from the riverside walk to the house (left).**

The instant garden

The difficulties of the small suburban back garden are familiar to Julian Treyer-Evans: he has one himself, at the back of his semi-detached home. But as a garden designer he believes in having fun and enjoyment, rather than hard slog, in the garden.

Ingenuity and inventiveness are the mark of his skill. That's why TV personality Anna Ford chose him to design her garden. And for Anita Roddick, the founder of Body Shop, he invented (at her request) what is probably the only *funny* designer garden. Jokes included a permanently jumping fish, golden stones leading through the orchard to the end of a rainbow, and a back to front sundial.

But there is also a dizzily romantic rose garden, in pink and white and blue to match the sitting room nearby, a Japanese garden, a green and white barbecue area and a formal water garden – as well as the jokes.

In his designer gardens, he gives traditional ideas a new twist. A pergola for roses or climbing plants is painted green at the bottom and blue at the top to fit in with grass and sky. Paving isn't just paving: it could be alternating granite sets and gravel squares like a crossword puzzle. Paths are tapered at the end to make them look longer. Lawns are put at different levels.

Pergolas, paving, paths and lawns are traditional to gardens – but Julian Treyer-Evans uses them in an untraditional way.

● **Julian Treyer-Evans redesigned this garden from scratch in just four months, working by himself at weekends just like any ordinary gardener.**

In his own back garden at Hurst-pierpoint, Sussex, he has used almost all these ingredients. The pergolas at the back are painted blue to increase the distance, and are used to hide the shed and greenhouse tucked away behind them. His lawn has three different levels – highest in the middle, then lower again at the far end. The patio has paving squares cut at the corner to insert a small coloured concrete lozenge to make it look more interesting. This transformation of a dull back garden with a crazy paving path and a concrete rock garden up one side took only four months.

'People won't wait for years to see results nowadays,' he says. 'They move houses quite often so they want to see results soon enough to enjoy them'.

Unlike some gardening experts he's neither snobbish nor stuffy. He's probably Britain's only designer who actually *likes* gnomes though he's not yet used them in any of his designs. He took up garden designing after a spell in the army, followed by three years at Merrist Wood Horticultural College.

He aims to be practical in his approach. As a family man he wants a garden, and a large lawn, where he can spend time with his children. 'I had to stop myself putting in too many ideas. As a designer I had so many.'

There are no curves in his garden. 'I like formality and order in the garden for the framework. I'm very fond of straight lines rather than curves.' He enjoys the formality of French gardens.

● **View from the patio.**

● **Borrowed landscape from the playing fields.**

If his clients ask for a traditional English country garden, with double herbaceous borders, shrub roses and masses of plants, he will oblige them. 'But I think that gardens like Great Dixter and Sissinghurst are for people who love gardens and spend a lot of time in them. They require endless maintenance.' That 1930s style does not suit people without much time to spare, he feels. 'I don't think people should have to spend too much time working too hard in their gardens: they should have time to enjoy them. That's why I always encourage people to put loads and loads of mulch on their gardens. It means much less weeding.'

Unexpectedly, he's not a paving or gravel enthusiast. Yes, he will use both, and feels that they should be made 'as interesting as possible'. But he feels that lawns have an important part to play. 'A lovely lawn makes such a difference, even if the garden otherwise is a bit of a mess. You can dish them slightly to make them more interesting. It makes the whole lawn look larger. Or you can do split level lawns to make them look longer and more interesting.'

His own garden is overshadowed by a large walnut tree. 'I pruned a lot off

it because its branches originally came down to the lawn. The squirrels sit up on it eating walnuts throwing down the shells below. You need a helmet during autumn as protection!'

Wildflower gardens, another current fad, are not much to his taste. 'But I do like wildlife in the garden. So I have planted the inside of the pergolas with shrubs, wild strawberries, raspberries and even brambles so that the insects and birds have lots to eat'.

He has also installed garden lighting. 'There's one to highlight the tree and two others to light the garden near the steps. I think lighting is very important and people tend to neglect it.'

Down the shady side of the garden he has planted lots of yellowy variegated plants. On the sunny side there is a mixed border of roses and perennials with an evergreen framework.

Small careful touches make maintenance easier. The borders are retained by a edging of concrete bricks, which are an inch lower in height than the lawn. A little three-inch ditch separates lawn from brick – to stop the grass growing over the brick and make mowing more easy. One of the little box hedges that he loves so much is growing between the patio and the lawn. It will stay low – only a foot long but it will be cut so that it hides the fact that the whole garden slopes at an angle to the left.

And right at the back of the garden comes a cheeky Treyer-Evans idea. He has taken down the fence that separates his garden from the nearby play-

● **Different lawn heights add distance (left). The view towards the house (right).**

ing field, and merely placed an Edwardian white bench there instead – thus borrowing (as it were) the landscape to extend his garden view.

But like so many other people who have to work for a living he hasn't yet had time to do all he'd like. 'I haven't got the planting quite right yet,' he says, surveying the garden which he has made entirely at weekends without any extra labour. 'It still needs the small touches that make a garden really fine. I understand why so many people want an instant garden. Why shouldn't they treat the garden like the house and redecorate every so often? But as a designer I try to help them to a happy medium – a garden that will look good from the beginning but last some time too.'

Instant gardening techniques are much in demand now that working people change houses every four-and-a-half years, according to one survey. The pace of modern living, which

means moving to where work is available, doesn't suit the old style of gardening. Waiting for twenty years or so to develop a good garden is just not practical. Garden designers like Julian Treyer-Evans recognise this. 'If you want to make a garden in a few months, rather than a few years, what you need to do is to see what's there already and make use of it. If there are mature trees, build them into the design. If there are well-grown shrubs, use them too. You can move almost any plant, as long as you give them plenty of water during the move and for several weeks afterwards.'

However pressed for time you are, spend some of it making a plan or ask a designer to do one for you. It will turn out quicker in the long run, if you know what you are doing. If you are uncertain about it, then lay your brickwork edging without concrete so you can change it if you don't like what you see.

Buying mature shrubs and trees can be difficult, and is always expensive. Ordinary garden centres often don't stock them. The temptation therefore is to choose fast growing plants like Leyland cypress which then grow like giants to become a pest in a few years time.

'Plants like good soil, so the more you can improve it and the less competition there is from weeds, the faster they will respond. Dig in lots of well rotted manure. Keep watering through the summer. The first year you'll pray that the new plants will grow quickly: two years later you will be praying they stop growing!'

Shrubs that grow quickly, if you

treat them well, include the *Cornus alba* species, escallonias, hebes, and *Eleagnus x ebbingei*. Fast-growing yellow-leaved plants are *Lonicera nitida* 'Baggesen's Gold' and yellow privet, *Ligustrum ovalifolium* 'Aurea'. The last two could also be used as hedging.

But for really beautiful hedges Julian Treyer-Evans prefers yew, despite its reputation for being slow growing. 'Leyland cypress hedges may serve a purpose but yew has much more dignity. If you give it good treatment it grows much faster than most people imagine. You can sometimes buy fairly large yew plants too. Its dark green colour and close texture also make it an excellent background for other plants.'

Instant cover for eyesores includes masses of ivy plants or *Clematis montana*. 'Russian vine is probably too rampant,' warns Julian. 'You can also cover an eyesore with a *trompe l'oeil* painting. I've seen a blank wall painted to look as if there are steps leading into it with hedges either side and a garden beyond. It looked wonderful.'

For an instant lawn, buy turf instead of seed. If you have a lawn already in the garden in bad condition, bring it back into health by killing the weeds and feeding it with a combined chemical at regular intervals throughout the summer. 'It's wonderful what that will do.'

For the flower borders Julian recommends fast growing and reliable perennials like *Achillea ptarmiga* 'The Pearl', *Achillea millefolium* 'Cerise Queen' and the big spurges like *Euphorbia robbiae* or *wulfenii*. Fill in with bedding plants like Busy Lizzies, petunias and dwarf mallows.

Finally, use containers to fill in any awkward bits and provide colour, while the shrubs are growing. 'Empty them out in winter and put in fresh soil. Fill them with winter pansies for colour, then bulbs or primula in spring, and finally bedding plants.'

Peculiar to all successful gardens wherever they are in the world, whether they are ancient or modern, large or small is that they adhere to the basic principles of design. To be successful they must be unified so that the plants, the hard materials and the overall design itself have a sense of harmony and tranquillity. The garden must also have a sense of balance and scale.

Designing gardens has led to my travelling all over the world. The more one travels the more one sees, the more people one meets the more ideas fill one's mind. It is exciting but it can be confusing. The art of design is the ability to assimilate these ideas, to use the appropriate ones and above all, to keep everything simple. This is the last and perhaps the most important principle. Remember this and one just cannot go wrong.

Julian Treyer-Evans

● **Geraniums, petunias and fuschias frame the steps up to the greenhouse (left).**

Town gardens – inside and out

Exotic long white flowers of angel's trumpets and other Mediterranean climbing flowers hang from the walls of Susan Gernaey's tiny conservatory. For while other garden designers extend the house into the garden with the room outside look, Susan Gernaey takes the garden into the house. What makes her conservatory look so special are the plants. The structure itself is nothing more than a simple lean-to shape without any particularly elaborate design trimmings. The flowers and foliage inside are everything.

Outside too scores of rare plants flourish in the small back garden – many of them plants which will be

● **The exquisite little town garden with the English country garden look (below). Susan Gernaey in her conservatory (right).**

taken inside the conservatory in winter. It is a kind of plantswoman's tiny paradise surrounded by the bricks and concrete of London.

Not for her the masses of paving and half dozen low maintenance shrubs that mark the yuppie garden designer, anxious to use the garden for cocktails, barbecuing, sitting in – anything but gardening. Quite the reverse. She has created an elaborate little garden in Battersea, complete with lawn and little box balls.

'My garden is really a collection of plants,' she says. 'I haven't even counted them up but I know that I have an enormous variety of plants here, in just forty square feet. I think I am as much a botanist as a garden designer!'

At the moment she designs mainly London gardens. 'My ideal client is one who starts off knowing nothing and trusts me, and then ends up as a passionate gardener,' she says. 'I'd much rather work for clients who are enthusiastic about plants than people who don't give a damn.'

She came to gardening designing ten years ago, after some years in the fashion business followed by interior design. 'I think the most important thing in life is that you should enjoy your work, and I was always very keen on gardens. I love plants.' People who love plants will love her gardens. TV presenter Sarah Kennedy and Miriam Karlin, the actress, both have a Susan Gernaey garden. Miriam's is a shady town garden which needed care in the choice of its plants.

● **The view through the conservatory door (left) towards the sweet peas, and (right) lilies and blue agapanthus.**

Unlike most designers, Susan does a lot of conservatory design, planting indoors as well as outdoors for people. Her own conservatory has the plantswoman's approach. Though it has good heating, blinds for shading and protecting plants from the sun, and very good ventilation, there is no elaborate staging or furniture. The beauty comes from the plants inside. They produce the colour and excitement, like living indoor decor. Wonderfully exotic flowering climbers crawl up the simple white walls. There are two kinds of passion flower, one with a charming pink flower, the other a strange green and white flower but with as much as two and a half pounds of fruits in late summer.

'I specialise in Mediterranean plants in here which go out in their pots in the summer. I'm also very fond of plants with fruit,' she says. A particularly striking conservatory plant is the variegated lemon tree, which even produces variegated fruits, striped green and yellow. But there is also a tangerine tree, which like all citrus trees, has a mixture of mature orange fruit, small green fruit and white scented flowers all through the year. 'Grapevines are also fun. I pick four bunches of grapes a year from mine, which are Muscat of Alexandria and Black Hamburg.' With conservatories back in fashion as a way of extending living space into the garden, Susan Gernaey specialises in helping people with plants for them. It's not nearly as easy as most people think. 'The most common mistake is to assume that plants like the same conditions as people. They don't. So those glass extensions which are just part of the living room aren't necessarily good for growing plants.'

Plants don't like central heating or the high level of heat that we enjoy in our homes. The only plants that will survive in the same conditions as human beings are office plants like rubber plants or houseplants like aspidistras. It helps therefore to have a conservatory which can be shut off from the adjoining rooms of the house.

'Most people don't realise that plants need air as well as light and water. One of the most important things for plants in a conservatory is having proper ventilation. You should have roughly one sixth of the floor area in roof or window ventilation,' she advises.

Thermostat controlled heaters help keep the conservatory frost-free, and automatic ventilators stop it getting too hot – both vital for many of the more unusual plants. But it does not have to be at a high heat. Her own conservatory falls to about 40° Fahrenheit without harming the plants inside it. 'It is possible to grow a great variety of plants thought to be tender in a comparatively cool conservatory,' she says.

Overwatering kills more plants than any other cause. 'I check each plant individually and in winter I cut down

● **Inside the conservatory lilies and white agapanthus in pots (right). More flowers in pots outside (left), including hostas in the distance.**

the watering radically. The other problem is pests. Plants must be fed, watered, ventilated, and kept free of pests. A conservatory creates ideal conditions for pests – all that warmth and shelter and low humidity!' Regular spraying is a must.

She recommends climbers for the conservatory, like plumbago, Star jasmine (*Trachelospermum jasminoides*), and the various passion flowers. Angels trumpets (*Datura cornigera* 'Knightii' is a double white fragrant variety) are relatively easy plants, as long as they are kept well watered. Jasmine polyanthum flowers in winter and spring. Geraniums and begonias will flower in a conservatory twelve months in the year, and will also survive underwatering though they need light. Morning glory, either the perennial, or the annual kind grown from seed, is also pretty.

Every single one of her conservatory plants looks healthy (which is more unusual than it sounds!). The lilies put out gigantic white blooms from their pots. The blue-flowered plumbago growing up the wall and the many geraniums in their pots all look well, unlike so many indoor plants.

Her regime is a strict one. The plants are sprayed with water every single day in summer. They are given a liquid feed of high potash fertiliser weekly,

● **The grey foliage of bushy *Convolvulus cneorum* next to a little stone ball on old bricks (left). A large trellis, trees and shrubs hide the surrounding Battersea buildings, giving a secluded atmosphere to the garden (right).**

repotted when necessary, and once a month all the pots are taken out onto the lawn and sprayed for pests.

Outside in the garden there are more fruit trees – a peach tree in a pot with fifteen peaches on it, and a fig tree. Both these live in the conservatory in winter. Tomatoes are growing up the wall, looking rather like exotic green climbers. There are pots and pots of lettuce-leaved basil, grown from seed bought in Italy.

Indeed there are 150 terracotta pots in all in the conservatory and garden. Sweet peas grow up a pyramid of canes in one pot: daisy-like *Erigeron mucronatus* in another; in a third are blue daisies (*Felicia ammelloides*). There are blue agapanthus lilies, white agapanthus, purple toadflax, myrtles and two large hostas – all in pots.

Her outside garden is simply a

square, lined with large trellis to hide any neighbouring tatty fences, with the lawn in a circular shape. Antique little stone balls on unmortared walls made of old London bricks lead from the terrace of York stone onto the lawn.

But, as Susan Gernaey says, the point of the garden is the plants. Among old favourites, such as hellebores and a white lacecape hydrangea, there are rarities like tree peonies, a paulownia tree with large leaves coppiced back every year to make good foliage, double red nasturtiums, a grey bushy plant confusingly named *Convolvulus cneorum*, lots of blue meconopsis poppies earlier in the summer, and an *Abutilon vitifolium* with dazzling lavender flowers in June.

'Planning what you will plant is like doing a jigsaw puzzle. You have to

think of so many things – the colour, when the flowers come, the foliage shape, the height of the plant, which direction the garden faces, and how to have something interesting throughout the year.'

'I work it all out on paper first,' she says. 'If I have made a plan, then I am quite happy to wait for the plants or to hunt around for them in special nurseries. It really pays off to do that, rather than just going to a garden centre and buying what's there just because it's in flower! Garden designing is actually very hard work. I consider it a luxury to work at what I love doing best. It's something that you can work at all your life.'

● **Mimosa and lilies flourish in pots, so do hostas (left and right).**

Every space however seemingly impossible can be made into a garden. Marjorie Fish starts her classic book Gardening in the Shade *'Some people think that to own a shady garden should be a matter for sympathy, but I always feel it is one for envy'. I agree with her. However, the smaller the space the greater the challenge. Town gardens are an extension of the house both practically and visually and can be treated like rooms, the 'furnishing' being done with plants, lawns, paving and brickwork. Scale is all important and dividing the garden into compartments will give a greater feeling of space. My perfect garden would be one with a formal design softened by luxurious planting.*

If you are thinking of designing your own garden, plan it very carefully first. It is difficult to anticipate how a garden will develop and although the structural framework will remain unchanged the plants will grow and mature. Visiting gardens regularly is a wonderful source of inspiration and, of course, there are scores of excellent gardening books for reference. Finally, do not design a garden which you will have to be a slave to, after all, gardening is supposed to be a pleasure!

Susan Gernaey

Edwardian elegance

As Savile Row is to suits, so Anthony du Gard Pasley is to gardens – a garden designer of impeccable discretion and traditional virtues. His design style is bespoke, matching the garden to the client, rather than the client to the garden. 'I would hate to think that somebody might go into one of my gardens and say to the owners, "I see you've had Pasley." What I am doing is to match the garden to the character of the owners. It's the essential part of my designing,' he says.

'And I am always discreet about my clients. I wouldn't dream of telling anybody who they are. All I could say is that they are country rather than town gardens, often on small country estates owned by landowners of a middling kind.'

His own garden in Tunbridge Wells, Kent, looks backwards to the age of Edwardian elegance. You most certainly would not want to have cocktails on the patio or use his garden as a room outside. You might on the other hand have tea in it – with an atmosphere suited to cucumber sandwiches and perhaps a parlourmaid in a starched uniform. 'I was determined to make the garden look back to 1910, the days before the First War,' he declares, as he sips tea on his terrace looking not unlike an Edwardian country gentleman.

It is a role he would be happy with. Not only is his garden Edwardian in atmosphere, but he wears a monocle, is an enthusiast for the Mapp and Lucia novels of E.F. Benson, and enjoys living in a house that once belonged to Queen Victoria's daughter, Princess Louise, who married the Marquis of Lorne.

At first he bought the whole huge house and garden for himself. Then later split it in two: leaving himself a half house and garden which are more than generous for one person living on his own. The interior decoration matches its nostalgic garden exterior – a re-creation of the principles of Gertrude Jekyll, who changed English gardens from a mass of bedding plants to a symphony of perennial flowers and shrubs. Its style fits neatly with the Victorian house with its remodelled 1920s facade. Indeed the beds of rhododendron, which came with the original

● **A shaft of real sunlight in the yellow front garden which is already planted to look sunny (left). The house (right) once belonged to Queen Victoria's daughter, Princess Louise, who was a close friend of the great garden designer Miss Gertrude Jekyll.**

house, may go back as far as Jekyll herself, who was a close friend of Princess Louise.

He has split the garden up into different 'rooms'. There is a winter garden at the dark side of the house, and facing north, in the front, a yellow garden which he describes as 'giving a feeling of warmth and sunlight.' The mixed rose and flower borders either side of a grass path in the main garden are full of silvery greys, pale pinks and mauves, and muted blues making up Anthony Pasley's nostalgic look back towards the Jekyll days.

'I have chosen soft subtle colours to lead up to the view. Strong colours would distract the eye from looking beyond and I want people to look beyond. I have borrowed the landscape for my garden, which is particularly important if you have a small garden to start with.' Today he has more view than normal – because the hurricane of 1987 blew down a huge Monterey pine, a mature magnolia, and one or two other trees were damaged from the little wood on the far end of his garden. In three-quarters of an acre, this was a big loss.

Not for Anthony Pasley a low maintenance garden, which would not fit in with the Edwardian style. His garden is full of small labour-intensive touches –

● **The front garden (above and below, right) faces north, and catches the late sun. It is planted with shrubs like golden privet, box and lonicera and perennials like bronzed fennel and yellow balm. At the side a golden hop makes an entrance archway. (far right) The golden garden again with creeping Jenny and yellow variegated *Eunonymous fortunei.***

like the cotoneaster which is trained under each of the stone steps leading down from the Italianate terrace, with its Edwardian garden furniture, to the main lawn.

The basic design of the garden is one of formality, with the occasional simple curve to lead the eye into the view. 'I hate waggly curves. I can't stand gardens that waggle or snake about for no good reason. Curves should always be creative – designed either to lead the eye outwards or to make a natural transition from one area to another. My garden is meant to look very *degagé*. But it requires an extreme amount of contrivance. It's a complicated use of hardy plants.'

'I am lucky to have a very very good gardener one day a week. Otherwise I really couldn't manage. I look after a garden in Luxembourg and have done one in Spain – and am busy with another in the South of France. So I have to be ready to take off any time. I just wish I had time to do more here.'

When the EEC harmonises its economic affairs in the 1990s, Anthony Pasley will be ready for it. He has considerable experience with gardens

● **Anthony on the terrace (left). Cotoneaster is trained under each stone step leading to the lawn (below).**

abroad – where he creates English gardens among the prevailing continental parterres. In Luxembourg they find his herbaceous borders amazing. 'The trouble in doing gardens abroad is getting the plants. I do have rather a rich palette of plants, which I use in seemingly natural but in fact highly contrived groups. I can't always find what I want in nurseries in Europe.'

His flower borders are a good example of this. Among the old roses like 'Nuits de Young', the pink and white 'Rosa Mundi' and 'Hebe's Lip' with white petals tinted red, he has planted unusual mop-headed willows *(Salix helvetica)* grown rather like rose standards punctuating the border. 'They'll probably become a cliché soon but I needed four plants to punctuate the border and I saw these,' he says. There are even wild plants like a tall herb Robert and pink self seeding corncockles. 'By growing unusual plants I get to learn about them. It's no good just seeing a plant at a show or in a catalogue and then getting it for a client. I have to grow them myself to know what they will really be like.'

He is fond of odd juxtapositions – a *Clematis alpina* with blue flowers followed by seedheads grows through cotoneaster with pink flowers that are followed in the autumn by orange berries – and a wild purple knapweed grows amid the catmint. 'I like little jokes like that.'

● **Looking down the garden to a borrowed landscape. The left hand border is full of greys and pinks (left). A clever juxtaposition: pink clematis grows through copper beech (right).**

When not designing gardens, he lectures at the English Gardening School in Chelsea Physic Garden, where he is co-principal and like so many other designers writes books. His most recent, written with Rosemary Alexander, is *The English Gardening School,* a guide to planning and planting a garden.

His garden is full of scented flowers. 'I think it is very important,' he says. 'Unlike a lot of men I like very strong scents. I even like lilies inside the room.' Drifts of regale lilies at the bottom of his garden fill the surrounding air with their powerful perfume.

An Anthony Pasley garden, from the original design plan right through to the finished garden, does not come cheap. 'When I started getting too much work, I put my fees up enormously thinking it would fall off. But it just encouraged people. Of course when people call in a designer, they are buying experience, a good many years experience, and all the knowledge that has accumulated in those years. It's not like getting a design out of a book. All my gardens are specially tailored to the personality of the owner.' That, above all, is the Pasley philosophy. 'Colour is one of the most important techniques in making a garden', says Anthony Pasley.

The mistake most gardeners make is to use too many colours in the first place, and to mix them all up. Each colour nullifies the one next to it and one colour quarrels with the next one. I wish seed merchants wouldn't sell these packets of mixed colours.'

Unlike some designers, he believes that there is no such thing as a bad colour. The oranges and yellows now out of fashion with gardening snobs are as good as the pinks and whites so popular in herbaceous borders. 'There is no such thing as a bad colour. You've just got to know how to deal with it. I grow a psychedelic orange rose against purple-leaved beech and it looks wonderful.' But for people less certain, the safest thing is either to have a single colour theme or to use colours based on blue or yellow.

'When you think about it, all flower colours are based either on blue or yellow. The blue range includes hard whites, all the bluish pinks which one finds in old fashioned roses, crimsons, reds and purples and the associated foliage. The yellow range includes warm whites, creams, all the orange pinks like salmon and apricot, orange and the scarlet red.'

In his front garden he uses bright yellow shrubs like golden privet, yellow box and lonicera, golden conifers and golden euonymous. Smaller plants like creeping Jenny, yellow balm and golden leaved water irises are mixed with grey plants like silver variegated kerria or *Senecio greyi.* These yellows give the impression of reflected sunlight, so they are a good colour to plant in places where the real sunlight is rare.

Yellow, orange and reds also give an impression of heat and warmth. 'I like using grey plants with yellow. The combination looks very good. People often try to soften colours by using, white. It doesn't work because white is a strong

● **Salmon pink geraniums and** *Cistus ladanifer*, **with a maroon spot on each white petal, which thrives on the terrace.**

colour in its own right. It's far better to use grey instead.'

White flowers need lots of variegated white and green foliage to make them less startling. Plants which have white flowers peering out of dark foliage can be too startling to work into a colour scheme.

To brighten a dark garden, he says, you must use pale colours like whites, creams and certain shades of clear mauve, rather than dark ones. The proper place for the brilliant colours is, ironically, the lightest part of the garden. Bright crimsons, oranges and pinks need lots of light to glow but just look muddy in dark places. Anthony Pasley says: 'Brightest scarlet changes into a kind of dead red in a dark spot.' Finally he advises his pupils at the Gardening School not to forget foliage colours.

● **Another view of the golden front garden showing the wide variety of foliage plants, re-echoing the theme of yellow, bronze and green.**

Many people assume that the boundary and the shape it creates on the ground are the beginning and the ending of a garden, but to me the most important factors lie outside. The skyline, whether it consists of distant hills or nearby rooftops, will always draw the eye and the design of the garden should recognise this fact, either by using complementary lines as a kind of linear echo or by the placing of objects to create a counterpoise. One can gain inspiration, too, from other things seen beyond the boundary, roads or rivers, the pattern of fields or the spacing of windows, some combination of which can be used in a way which will clearly link the garden to its surroundings. Only when these are totally unattractive should the garden seek to create an enclosed world and even then the gesture of a single upright tree may be sufficient to link this enclosure to the sky and its freely drifting clouds above.

While seeking to gain from the outside world, we must also remember what can be given in exchange. For every one who enters the gate, hundreds will pass by and their lives can be made more pleasant by a little forethought. It may be no more than hiding some intrusive drain pipes, planting a tree which will cast a shadow pattern to break the regularity of a boring street, or placing a group of golden crocus where they will catch the eye of commuters rushing for the morning train. It is often the small details which are not immediately obvious which count the most, and that is just as true in the garden as in any other aspect of life.

Anthony du Gard Pasley

Garden Ornaments

The stone pigs that snuffle their way through Michael Balston's garden are the designer alternative to garden gnomes – just as funny, less obtrusive and much more expensive. They are part of the inventive style of Britain's most highly qualified garden designer equally at home designing a funny stone pig or laying out a million-pound garden.

Michael Balston started his career as an architect, then qualified all over again as a landscape architect. He started work on giant projects like the Civic Centres of Hillingdon and Reading – working on a scale few other garden designers have experienced. 'I did one or two private gardens at that stage, and then I worked on the designs for the King of Saudi Arabia's garden in Bishop's Avenue. It was a very ambitious project,' he says with understatement about a garden which cost a seven figure sum. From there he went to Saudi Arabia where he designed gardens for Arabs living there. No mean achievement this – there is a strong Arab tradition of

valuing and enjoying gardens which means they recognise both talent and lack of it.

At the end of the 1970s he came back to Britain and set up as a garden designer here. This isn't his only work – he remains a partner in an architectural firm, does some large scale commercial landscaping and also runs a garden ornament company. But it is as a garden designer he is best known with his partner Pen Linell.

His own garden in a Wiltshire farmhouse is 'a working laboratory for plants and furniture and stonework,' he explains. 'It's immensely useful to see how plants perform, though I have got far too many different kinds in here.'

He and his wife Meriel and their three young children moved in a few years ago. The garden was in a poor way, and the thatched wall and summerhouse at the back, which divides flower garden from vegetable patch, was derelict and had to be rebuilt. He has redesigned the flower garden in front completely. From the paving round the house, stairs lead up to the lawn and borders and above is a charming wooden arbour of his own design.

● **Michael Balston in his garden.**

His strong architectural approach is evident. In the middle of the lawn he has built a paved rectangular sitting area. The garden reaches vertically as well as horizontally. Flowerbeds either side grow upwards like a kind of frame – thanks to the four wooden pyramids with their old roses growing up the sides. The pyramids give a vertical dimension to the garden rather like topiary or walling. Made for clematis, rambling roses, sweet peas or any other climbers, these are one of Michael Balston's really beautiful garden ornaments. 'It's not a new idea. Pyramids like this have been around for about 500 years. I just redesigned a new version.'

He is reassuring about gardens. 'This garden is designed to accommodate weeds. Nobody nowadays has time to spend hours weeding. My entire philosophy is that weeds should exist in gardens, but if you pack the flowerbeds really full you don't notice them.' Like other designers he finds that a design sense lacking in many keen gardeners. 'Most enthusiastic gardeners look at detail rather than overall layout. They are bewitched by plants. In English gardens no design at all is more common than too much!'

Even though his design practice is at the upper end of the market Michael Balston does not puff up the role of garden designer. 'I hate the prima donna approach of some interior decorators and garden designers. I can't over-emphasise that a designer is just a link

● **Pink roses in front of *Hebe salicifolia* (left). The wooden furniture, designed by Michael Balston, enhances the garden's beauty (right).**

in the chain.' Imposing a design on a garden, without thoroughly involving the person who's going to pay and also the person (whether head gardener or the owner) who maintains the garden, is, in his view, unprofessional. 'You only have to look round so many of Britian's larger homes to see what happens when a garden design isn't kept up.'

There isn't a Michael Balston style – partly because of his insistence that each garden must be different. Despite working with wealthy clients, he is not in favour of too much formality. 'Too much symmetry is just unsophisticated,' he says.

The gardens he has designed for Chelsea have been noticeable for their originality – a pink and white garden for Fabergé was the first one to allow

● **Wooden pergolas give the garden a vertical dimension (left), and (below) little box hedges and cones.**

the public to walk round inside, rather than just look from outside. He talks of 'inflicting a little originality' on every garden he designs.

'Most of my work is fairly traditional. I get the impression that people think of gardens as a refuge from the modern things in life. They are seeking reassurance in the garden, so the design regrettably sometimes tends to be backward looking. I've done one or two really modern gardens – perhaps the most exciting one was a plan for a German garden which was going to have earth sculpture in it. I'd also love to do a garden pergola in chrome, for instance. I'm dying to do a high tech garden for someone.'

In his own garden, his choice is not at all high tech. Old roses, lilies, and fine perennial plants like the mauve *Campanula lactiflora* 'Loddon Anna'. Yew hedges, not yet fully grown, as well as surrounding walls, will make it into an enclosed refuge from the outside world.

He is modest about himself but pondering the difficulties of designing gardens, he remarks: 'My job is to see what isn't there. That's the easy part of designing a garden. The difficult thing is making it happen.'

Most of the garden ornaments on the market were either too small or too meanly detailed for Michael Balston, when he was designing a Chelsea garden for *Vogue* magazine a few years ago. So he started his own firm, producing well-designed garden ornaments in stone and wood. It's typical of his

● White *Lychnis coronaria* and clibming rose 'Sander's White' (left). Wooden pyramids frame the paved area (right).

approach that when he wrote a book about garden design he called it *The Well-Furnished Garden*. The best known of his ornaments are the pigs – made with polyester resin so strong that they can be lifted up by their little round tails. He has also produced urns, pedestals, obelisks and balustrading for the garden. For those with grander ideas he can provide a classical Bacchus in reconstituted stone marble or bronze.

Ordinary gardeners often forget that garden furniture is part of the overall garden look. A white plastic chair planted in the middle of an otherwise beautiful garden will blight all the beauty round it. Michael Balston prefers wood – his own designs. 'I got fed up with the lack of style and lack of weight and stability in timber furniture. I needed a big seat at the end of a London garden and so I made a semi-octagonal one specially for it. Then I started to sell them.' He believes people should choose their ornaments and furniture with the overall garden design in mind. Formal statuary will look good in a formal garden, but out of place in a little cottage garden. Wooden half barrels will look too rustic for a formal garden, but painted Versailles boxes would look right in a formal setting.

Be aware of scale. The ornament has to look in scale with the rest of the garden. Small statues in a huge garden will get lost. Never use too many ornaments. Use a garden ornament to create a focal point in the garden, but do be

● *Penstemen hartwegii* 'Garnet' and *Sidalcea malviflora* 'Rose Queen' with the summerhouse behind (left). One of the pyramids with lilies, foxgloves, and pink roses (right).

careful how you place it. Too low or too high and it will be missed altogether. Aim at having it at eye level.

Urns and pineapples need lots of plants falling round them, otherwise they look too posed. Put plants round their bottom, as well as planting the urns with floppy informal plants. The best way to get a statue covered with moss is just to leave it for a year under a tree, where the atmosphere is damp and shady.

You don't have to spend a lot of money on ornaments, though it helps. The white plastic urns that look so out of place in most gardens can be painted an earth or terracotta colour to blend in with the garden – though they still don't feel right when you touch them. Michael Balston also suggests using natural objects. 'You could have a natural rock as an ornament or a pile of pebbles. Other alternatives are chimney pots, half barrels, pots, urns or stone balls.'

● **Michael Balston uses herbs like borage, here in front of yellow broom, and fennel on the left (left).** *Achillea* **'Moonshine' (below) and (right) a Triton mask.**

Having come into garden design from architecture, I suppose it is inevitable that I tend to concentrate on the spaces of the garden, and the structure that forms them, before getting too deeply involved in the choice of plants. The opportunities for making spaces largely depend on what the site offers in the way of existing buildings, aspect, slope, and so on, so it is vital to study the site well. Spaces will then be formed to satisfy a variety of functional needs, to respond to buildings or perhaps to take advantage of a view.

The formation of these spaces implies a degree of enclosure by surrounding elements, and these might be walls, fences, or trellis. Or enclosure might be created by the use of plants – trees, hedges, shrubs, borders and so on. It is the combination of space and enclosure in all its variety that begins to bring magic into a garden. It is perhaps only then that plants as individuals really begin to tell.

Plants never cease to amaze me with their beauty, their changing forms and colours and each year I learn how to use a few more. In a sense, they are the decorative scheme that reinforces the space, and one can draw useful analogies with the way one decorates and furnishes a house. They are seldom at their best as unrelated individuals – it pays to think of them in groups that respond both to their neighbours and to their space. That is not to say that they cannot exist in isolation or out of place – they can and do, and frequently and most charmingly, by mistake.

Michael Balston

OUTDOOR ROOMS

Outdoor rooms

Gravel and paving with unusual plants growing through them is the mark of landscape designer John Brookes – one of the first English designers to give gardens the 'room outside' look. His gardens are for living in, not just looking at.

Nothing could be further from country lawns and nostalgic herbaceous borders than a John Brookes garden. His particular designer look has turned its back on the nostalgia of Gertrude Jekyll and Vita Sackville West in favour of modern living.

As a garden designer he is resolutely practical. Bricks, gravel and even concrete slabs have replaced the hideously expensive York stone. Low maintenance plants like euphorbias take over from the traditional perennial pretties which take so much care to grow.

'I started in the sixties at the end of the Duchesses and *House and Garden* era,' he says. 'People with titles were too hard up to have their gardens designed, and so I did the gardens of those who today would be called yuppies.'

He made his name with small London gardens – the kind too urban and too tiny for the gardening snobs to notice. It took the Chelsea Flower Show twenty years or more to catch up with him and start showing courtyard small gardens as well as the traditional large garden sites.

His London gardens were a shock to the traditional gardeners, brought up to believe plants must come before everything else. You could sit in a John Brookes garden. You could hold a

● **The shapes of plants are as important as their colour (above). John Brookes in the gravelled walled garden with hostas and *Alchemilla mollis* (right).**

drinks party in it. And if you didn't like gardening, you could do very little gardening indeed. For he got rid of the shabby urban lawn with its white pigeon droppings and sad shaded grass in favour of cleaner dryer paving. And instead of trying to grow rambling roses and herbaceous perennials, he encouraged the tentative gardeners to have easy-care ivy, tough evergreen shrubs and perhaps a clump or two of blue grass. It was the Design Centre in your back garden and sheer bliss for the reluctant gardener. A John Brookes garden positively encouraged you to lie back in your garden lounger and enjoy it – rather than spending hours mowing and weeding.

From early in his career he taught others – at Kew, at the Inchbald School of Garden Design, first in London then in Teheran, where he studied Persian

gardens as well as teaching. When the Khomeini regime took power in Iran, he returned to England. Depressed with London, he moved to Fontwell in Sussex, where from a converted stables he opened the Clock House School of Garden Design running four-week courses within Denmans' Garden, using it as a setting and a kind of living library of garden ideas.

He took over the management of Denmans from its owner, Mrs Joyce Robinson a few years ago. The Sussex garden, which is three-and-a-half acres of plants grown in beds surrounded by gravel ground cover, is now full of John

Brookes touches. This large country garden has softened his designer look and given him the chance to use gravel on a larger scale. Plants grow in drifts out of pools of gravel and round sea-shore pebbles.

'I think it's wonderful to have gravel instead of muddy bits of lawn. It sustains the plants in winter because they are so well drained. It's the cold wet clay about their feet that kills them.'

While not forgetting the importance of strong design, he is a convert to what he calls 'the gravelly wildy look'. Now

● **Inside Denmans conservatory (left). Tall spikes of *Verbascum bombyciferum* and evening primroses (below), and (above) masses of Miss Willmot's ghost.**

that so many garden designers do his style of design with paving and easy plants, he has moved on. He is, as it were, neo-John Brookes, a more relaxed version of his former design style. 'I like jungles rather than borders and I like playing plant against plant. I don't want that specimen look – that 'plonkety plonk' look where each plant is on its own.'

Nowadays the gardens he designs are often in the United States. The Chicago Botanical Gardens chose him to design their English garden recently – an honour indeed. A Californian landscape design professor has summed up the John Brookes look as 'a contrast between geometry and nature'.

Plants, rather than the designer hardware of paving, are now what interest him most. 'Not flowers necessarily. I'm as much into foliage as flowers, though I haven't forsaken my love of pattern and shape.' The flowerbeds at Denmans

show this love. Foliage plants like the dark red berberis, blue eucalyptus, yellow yew, juniper and box abound. Shape is perhaps even more important than colour. Spiky plants like Scotch thistle, silvery white mulleins, yuccas, and phormiums rampage through the beds.

Where a single clump of blue grass once adorned his town gravel and paving outdoor room, today there is the natural drift of wild-growing self-seeding plants growing from an informal sea of gravel in Denmans. John Brookes the town designer has gone native in the country. The hard landscaper has at last succumbed to that very traditional English vice – a passion for plants.

The John Brookes style of garden planting means choosing plants in a different and exciting way. They are chosen not for scent or colour (though this comes into it) but for their part in the overall garden design. 'I tell most people to think of all the plants they want, and then cut down the number by half,' he says. 'They should use these fewer plants in bigger masses.'

To help use plants successfully in the garden, he divides them into five categories.

● Special plants. These are the plants which are going to have a special impact. Sometimes they are there already – like a tree growing in a London garden. The special plant can't fail to be noticed and the garden is planned round its impact. A silvery or a golden

● **Statue with _Acanthus mollis_ and giant hogweed (left). The Clock House School of Garden Design (right), with its 'outdoor-room' patio on the right.**

special plant could influence the colour scheme around it.

● Background or skeleton plants. These are the bones rather than the flesh of the garden – usually evergreen shrubs that will form the background throughout the year including winter. If a garden looks good in winter, it will look terrific the rest of the year.

● Decorative plants. These put colour and decoration into the garden often by foliage which lasts six months of the year while flowers only last a fortnight. Buddleias, philadelphus, hydrangeas, fuschias, and senecio have good shapes and can be grown in front of the background evergreens.

● Pretties. These are what their names suggest. In a John Brookes garden they would include *Alchemilla mollis,* sage, irises, hostas, one or two shrub roses and achilleas – all plants with interesting shapes and foliage rather than large bright flowers.

● Filling-in plants. These are bulbs and lilies that will come up and fill up spaces then die back again – summer hyacinths, lily-flowered tulips, *Galtonia candicans,* and of course lilies themselves.

'Most people start with the pretties and the fillers and work backwards. The trick of getting good garden planting is to start with the specimen plants first and then work your way in order down to the pretties and the bulbs. It works much better.'

Gravel is the cheapest way to get a hard surface on any garden. It's also the most informal – you can grow plants anywhere you choose through it. 'Gravel is well drained. It's wonderful to generate plants in,' says John Brookes.

'You can just get a spike, make a hole in it, and start off the plant that way.' You can also use a combination of gravel and paving – for instance, mock York stone squares used like stepping stones in a sea of gravel, or islands of several paving squares used to place a pot or sundial on.

To stop the gravel getting on the lawn or on flowerbeds, you need some kind of permanent edging. At the Clock House at Denmans, brick paving, placed on its side, is used. Never have gravel right near the house otherwise it just treads in on shoes. Lay some paving between the door and the gravel.

When making a new path, excavate out at least three inches. Then lay down binding gravel, the kind which has not

been washed too clean. The silt and clay among the gravel help it to compact down. There must be enough put down so that after it has been rolled the gravel on the path is about half-an-inch lower than the path's permanent edging. Roll it and consolidate it. Over this lightly sprinkle pea gravel, washed gravel of uniform size that looks attractive. Roll that in. To keep the gravel looking good, it has to be rolled regularly, otherwise it tends to distribute itself in an irregular way.

If the path is slightly humped in the middle this will allow water to drain

● **Denmans garden borders are winding streams of plants grown in large pebbles (left), and (above) foliage in gravel — very John Brookes.**

down into the sides. Rolling and con-
solidating it at the edges working
towards the middle should produce this
effect. Leave some open joints in the
path edging to let the water drain away,
otherwise the path will become a pond
after rainfall. For drives, rather than
paths, binding gravel can be used on its
own. But in order to get a really firm
driveway it would be best to use a
mechanical roller, not just a hand roller.

You can use chippings for colours
like white, grey, pinks or speckled. The
Elizabethans used different coloured
gravels in their knot gardens – so there
is a historical tradition. The disadvan-
tages are that they are sharp edged. But
because the chippings are angular they
support weight better. But be warned,
some of the colours can look rather like
cemetery graves.

Denmans Garden even uses big
pebbles from the beach to give an
impression of a dry stream. Plants love
it. It protects them from the cold, and
also keeps their roots well drained.

'You've got to be in the right frame
of mind for gravel. You must want a
rambly look. Weeds do seed themselves
on it, but they're easily pulled up after
rain. It's gravel rather than paving that
gives the rambling informal look.'

If you are lucky, your local gravel pit
may have some large pebble-sized
gravel. It's not sold in large quantities
but you may be allowed in to pick the
pebbles you want off the stockpile.

To buy gravel in very small quantities
you can get hundredweight bags.
Builders merchants sell these and also
loads of gravel up to half a ton. If you
want a ton or over, get it in a lorry load
from your local gravel pit. To work out
the quantity, multiply the length of the
path by the width and by the thickness
of the gravel in cubic metres. As gravel
is sold by weight a rough rule of thumb
is that two tons are about a cubic metre
of binding gravel. But as the density
varies, it is probably a good idea to
check with the local supplier.

● **The variegated leaves are more
important than flowers (right), and
(below) oriental poppies.**

I feel that a strong basic design for a garden is necessary wherever it is located, either in town or country, and the looser the planting of it the more the design aspect is necessary to hold the concept together. For the dividing line between what I feel is a lovely ramble, and what you might consider a mess, is very fine.

The design may be traditional and formal, although few have houses with these features, or it may be looser in concept. It will still have balance, however, though it might be asymmetric. I believe that this new look is now very much suited to many peoples' location and to the general mood and concern for wild flowers, for conservation and for domestic architecture. It also suits a more relaxed lifestyle, with for many, huge alternative interests to those of their garden; for if there are clumps of weeds amongst their herbs and gravel planting we simply call them natives!

It is no accident that some of the greatest works of gardening art, the most innovative and the most beautiful, have been made, designed and maintained by the same person, or more often two or three people working closely together as a team, each deeply committed to the outcome and with a similar version of the ideal. This was true of Hidcote, Sissinghurst, Bodnant, Crathes, Knightshayes, Sezincote, Kiftsgate and others. Professional designers can be part of this process but their ideas can only succeed in the long term with the understanding and the enthusiasm of those who run the place.

When you are designing your garden, think of it in different time-scales. Start by giving plenty of room to long-term heirlooms that you hope to pass on to your children or your successor. Go on to place the shrubs, especially evergreens, that will form the medium-term structure of the garden and finally pack out between with plants for quick effect which are expendable or can be easily moved and manipulated.

John Brookes

Water in the garden

Anthony Paul's gardens are Hollywood in green – dramatic settings with startling large green plants rather than flowers, water whenever possible with wooden decking like a stage above it. These are gardens with glamour – unrestrained, dramatic and not at all English. No wonder theatre people love them. The composer Andrew Lloyd Webber has had two Anthony Paul gardens, Gillian Lynne the choreographer has one, and Cameron Mackintosh the impresario has a fine one just on the edge of Regents Park.

Anthony's own garden is no exception. He has turned an Elizabethan black and white cottage into an English version of a Malibu beachhouse or a jungle longhouse. Not for him the traditional York stone patio, instead he has wooden decking out over a lake. It is unashamedly modern in mood.

Anthony Paul was brought up in New Zealand and started a career in fashion design before switching to landscape design. But it wasn't until he went into business with architect John Duane in 1983 that he was able to give his dramatic garden designs full scope.

'When I came back to England from New Zealand and Australia, I missed the banana plants, and all the tropical plants which grew near Sydney where I lived. I looked for dramatic plants which would take their place.

'We English are constipated by our forefathers. We all copy the past in our gardens. I think we should look at new ideas and new concepts. With modern buildings we should match our landscapes to them. We've done it with interiors, why not exteriors?'

His own garden is six-and-a-half acres of lakes, streams, woodland and vistas. The conventional option in his part of Surrey would have been rhododendrons and azaleas when he took over the jungle of brambles and neglected streams. 'I don't like rhododendrons anyway,' he says. Not for him the imitation of the National Trust's Nymans. Instead he dug out lakes – one just near the house – and planted them with dramatic swathes of big leaved perennials. There are hundreds of *Ligularia dentata* 'Desdemona' along the banks of the lakes, their round leaves bronzed underneath, simply crushing out any competing weeds. In the same way he grows great swathes of round-leaved

● A gigantic *Gunnera manicata* (below). John Duane, Anthony Paul and Harper by the lake (right).

Peltiphyllum peltatum, Petasites hybridus, the native butterbur and its Asian cousin, *Petasites japonicus* – perennial plants so unusual in gardens that most reference books ignore them.

'I try to create a landscape which has drama. I love the way plants explode into life. I think herbaceous borders are completely unnatural, against the rules of associating plants. Nature doesn't grow one plant at a time. I go back to nature and grow plants in great sweeps.'

For colour he grows meadow cranesbill along the lakeside near the house, and in other parts of the garden he sows water forget-me-nots among buttercups, or lets large patches of herb Robert grow among the longer grass.

Part of the impact comes from the sheer numbers involved – yards and yards of plants make even ordinary plants like hostas look wildly dramatic. Part comes from the choice of plants – *Nicotiana sylvestrias,* the Argentine version of the ordinary tobacco plant which grows six feet tall, and the simply gigantic rhubarb-like *Gunnera manicata.*

Most controversial of all is his use of giant hogweed, otherwise known as *Heracleum mantegazzianum,* a plant with the reputation for being a kind of Triffid – relentlessly advancing leaving human casualties in its wake. Giant hogweed haters round

● **Dramatic bamboos and gunnera (above, right). Giant hogweed down the drive (right). Wooden decking round the house with more jungle foliage (far right).**

Britain have written to plead with Anthony Paul to keep their enemy out of his gardens. In his own garden he has a hogweed drive, where the plants tower above entering cars with their 12-foot high flowerheads like gigantic cow parsley. 'It's quite safe to use them,' he says defensively. 'As long as you cut off the flowerheads before they seed, they can't spread. Decapitation is the key.' Ecological disaster or not, the giant hogweeds make surprisingly lovely cut flowers for the wooden decking round the house. 'I use wooden decking instead of stone because it's much warmer to the feet, and it's also half the price.'

Everywhere you look in his garden are vistas – usually with a piece of sculpture at the end. For he and his wife Hannah run a kind of outdoor sculpture gallery with everything from formal busts through hovering bronze birds to large ceramic pots.

There is none of the restrained understatement of the English garden. But then Anthony Paul does not prize understatement. He and his partner John Duane are gloriously uninhibited – one of their most amazing projects was to build a kind of tropical glasshouse onto an Elizabethan house.

His gardens are not for the shy, the discreet or the traditional but for glorious extroverts. John Duane puts it this way – 'He designs gardens like others design stage sets.'

Almost every garden from the Duane Paul Design Team, as the two partners call themselves, has water somewhere in it. 'Water is an attraction, a draw card. It is a magnet which makes people walk into the garden to

● **Wooden decking makes a sitting area and an outdoor balcony (left). The garden is adorned by outdoor statues from the Hannah Peschar gallery (above).**

look at it.' And Anthony Paul's book, *The Garden Design Book*, gives many different water ideas. Even if you don't have much money, spend it on good pond liner, a butyl sheet that will last for years. You can use the liner not just for a pond, but for a bog garden round its edge.

'Put your pond as close to the house as possible – not down the other end of the garden,' he advises. 'Then all the little bits of life in it, like goldfish, tadpoles and frogs, will give you pleasure all through the year. You can look at them through the window.'

Make your water feature as big as possible. Width is more important than depth (except from the point of view of fishkeeping), because the bigger the water surface the more reflections. 'Try to stretch the water from boundary to boundary, if you can. Then cross it with a bridge,' he says. 'The simplest bridge would just be a couple of railway sleepers.'

'The most important thing is to hide the edge of the liner,' points out John Duane. 'If you don't it looks terrible. You can use turf, or stones, or rocks over the edge, or you can use wooden decking. You just glue the liner to it. You also need to hide the liner just under the water level at the pond margin. The easiest way to do this is to have a shallow edge to the pond and put some soil and gravel there, out of which you grow plants.'

Water in the garden doesn't have to be a conventional pond. You can have an arrangement of wet pebbles, a millstone with water bubbling up the middle, or even a raised round pool to look like an old well. You could

have a stone trough full of water with a small submersible pump to keep the water moving. Or you could experiment with pots of water. Anthony Paul grows Typha reeds in soil covered with three inches of water in ceramic pots – a kind of containerised bog garden. Canna and arum lilies will also grow this way. In the winter take your mobile bog garden into the house or into a warm greenhouse to protect it from frost.

Japanese garden ideas influence his designs, and he has a Japanese hot tub sited over the lake, looking like a larger version of a barrel cut in half. In fact, thanks to some expensive plumbing you can boil your body in the tub, with the added pleasure of looking out over the lake at the same time. These Japanese versions of the jacuzzi are made by David Fletcher. 'You can bathe in it when snow is on the ground – because the water is hot enough to keep you warm,' he says. 'You're not even cold when you get out because of the heat from the bath. Children love them. We have one in our garden and my two boys always

● **Further down the garden a wooden bridge leads to even wilder territory (left). Anthony Paul brings fun and glamour into the gardens he designs. He is fond of round leaved plants like *Peltiphyllum peltatum*, *Petasites hybridus*, and *Petasites japonicus*. 'The arrangement of the plants make all the difference.' Round the house he grows rare plants like typha reed and ferns in pots (right). 'Ferns are my passion.' In summer he adds unusual bedding plants like *Nicotiana sylvestris* and grown out chicory with tall blue flowerspikes.**

splash about so much that it is half empty by the time they get out. That's the great advantage of hot tubs outside instead of inside – the steam and the water don't matter.'

The tubs come complete with tub, filtration equipment, heater and everything else you need, and can be large enough for four people at a time.

You need not plumb a hot tub into the garden if you want to save money. You can just fill it up with a garden hose. The water filter and disinfectant chemical will make sure that it is clean enough. The beauty of hot tubs is that they don't look like high tech. The natural wood cladding, either Douglas fir or teak, fits into the natural look of the garden. For designers like Anthony Paul, hot tubs are a way of bringing fun and luxury into the garden.

● **Near the house an artichoke plant is grown for its grey architectural foliage (left). Sculpture against the round leaves of *Ligularia dentata* (below).**

The key to a successful garden, whatever its size or location, is to recreate its natural habitat. This way, you avoid the overwhelming feeling that you are constantly struggling against the elements just to keep it under control. A more natural garden leaves you more time to observe and enjoy its features at your leisure. In my woodland, for example, I have bluebells, violets, primroses and wild orchids growing wild among the trees.

Large, informal areas of water and plants natural to the area not only make interesting features, pleasing to the eye, but are easy and economical to establish, and cut down tedious weeding and maintenance chores to a minimum.

Even so, every garden, no matter how beautiful or thoughtfully designed, needs reviewing on an annual basis. I target particular areas each year to give them a special lift and to create pockets of the garden that are always new and different. This might take the form of a new bridge, or a new design for a series of stepping stones or a bog garden.

Anthony Paul

Herbs for small gardens

Simon and Judith Hopkinson left London in the mid-seventies and decided to grow herbs in the country for a living. It was a romantic impulse but unlike most people in search of the good life, they managed to make a flourishing business out of it.

Now their herb nursery, Hollington, is one of the largest in the country and Simon Hopkinson designs herb gardens of all sizes – from tiny paved courtyards to long large herbaceous borders of herbs. Judith hunts out new herbs which are not just useful but ornamental too. Their herb garden designs are to be found as living example gardens in the huge old Victorian garden where they originally set up both home and business. A long double herb border, a garden for bees, a courtyard herb garden and many more can all be inspected and then a similar one bought – almost off the peg, as it were.

'Originally we just moved into the walled garden in a mobile home,' says Simon. 'We loved it. I'd been running a gardening contracting business in London and we just wanted to get away. You could open the door and walk out stark naked because the walls were so high.' Their friends thought they were mad to be living in a caravan with two children under five. The Hopkinsons had moments of doubt too – the first two years they did all the work themselves, sometimes digging or propagating until nearly midnight.

'We made a lot of mistakes.' says Simon, 'but I think we were in the right place at the right time. Herbs are part of the herby cottage feel to gardens that people now want.'

His first move into garden designing came in 1980 when they took a small stand at Chelsea. They designed a small patio with a herb border, which they made themselves. It won a silver medal. People wanted to buy not just the herbs but the garden itself. So from then on, as the Hopkinsons went on to win two gold medals at Chelsea, they also started offering gardens, not just individual plants. They will plant up an existing garden or design one from scratch.

'It just depends what people want. Usually people have just an area for herbs, not the whole garden, but they don't know how it should look. We will plan the plants for them for a herb border, for instance.'

If clients are not sure what they want, they can come and look round several sample gardens growing inside the nursery walls. The long double herb border was put in several years ago and the other gardens have followed, including one of their Chelsea Flower Show designs.

The beauty of the herbs themselves growing there is largely thanks to Judith Hopkinson who has made sure that the nursery sells beautiful varieties of the traditional herbs. You can get

● **Tall pink clary, yellow *Alchemilla mollis*, and *Rosa gallica* (below). Judith and Simon Hopkinson with Mint the tabby cat in the double herb border (right).**

startling red plantains, or ladybird poppies with a black inside to the petal, or big blue vipers bugloss as well as the traditional herbs.

'I looked out for herbs that were beautiful,' she says. 'After all, all the basic herbs are well known. But a lot of people want nice plants in their garden, and the fact that they are herbs is only secondary to them. They all have some use. It's taken me a long time to find some of them, for although they are all herbs they weren't in herb catalogues. For instance I don't think many people have variegated meadowsweet and most people wouldn't find vipers bugloss in a herb catalogue.'

Their long herb double border, 60ft with two beds of 8ft, is living proof that herbs need not be dull plants. There are the yellow showy daisy-like elecampane flowers, huge red orach rather like a giant ornamental sorrel, daisy-like feverfew (which is good for migraine), huge pink pokeroot from Egypt, silvery wormwood and yellow toadflax.

The herbs make good foliage plants too. Variegated elder, coppiced yearly, is a fine shrub. Tall caper spurge, yellow marjoram, variegated balm and small purple four-leaved clover all add shape and colour to the border.

'I love the way nature is partly responsible for this border,' says Simon Hopkinson. 'That red orach is self seeded from last year. I love its natural grouping. I think that's why women rather than men love herb gardens. Men hate things getting out of control!'

● *Salvia verticillata* and white goat's rue (left). Lavender and fennel in the stock beds (right).

● The Hopkinsons in the bee garden (left). Near the hive, on the left is red bergamot and meadow cranesbill. Right at the back is pink motherwort, *Nepeta camphorata*, blue vipers bugloss and variegated lemon balm. In the left foreground is *Geranium macrorrhizum.* (below) The knot garden.

They sell many wild plants. Their bee garden has a hive surrounded by plants which grow wild or are garden escapes in Britain – meadow cranesbill, pink motherwort, vipers bugloss, and pink *Geranium macrorrhizum*. 'A lot of herbs are natives anyway, or at any rate plants which were brought by the Romans. Of course, the very aromatic ones tend to be Mediterranean,' says Judith Hopkinson.

Also on sale are the tiny box plants, green and variegated, needed for knot gardens. Box pyramids and box balls

can also be found at their nursery. Indeed there is practically everything you could need, apart from paving, for a herb garden.

Herbs are tough growing plants most of which will grow happily in poor soil. 'Perhaps the only place where you couldn't have a comprehensive herb garden is somewhere in the shade or where it was too wet,' says Simon Hopkinson.

The traditional herb garden design mixes these plants with paving – which maximises the sun and also gives a good contrast between plants and design. 'Herbs are falling-about tumbling plants and paving gives them an element of order', he says.

The easiest herb garden of all is a chequer-board design. 'Just put a path round the herb garden, and leave an inner area of alternate stepping stones and planted pockets. 'It's a particularly good layout for culinary herbs, because you can get to them easily. Herbs like mint, which spread, are contained by the paving.'

A formal herb garden is usually square with a pool or a sundial in the middle. Four paths radiate from the centre which is paved, and then a circular path links the four.

'Knot gardens are probably the most expensive of the herb gardens. They need such a lot of plants'. The principle

● **Catmint and the knot garden with clipped hedging and a little box pyramid (left). A herbal water garden with white meadowsweet and gladwin (below).**

of a knot garden is to have a pattern laid out in little clipped hedges. The inside of each knot can be filled with plants or just left as a pattern with coloured gravels. Simon Hopkinson uses dwarf box both green and variegated, cotton lavender, and wall germander.

Each edging plant is put in four inches from the next and needs clipping regularly. As cotton lavender grows faster than box, it needs more frequent clipping. Just clip by eye, or if your eye isn't good use string attached to pegs to get the hedging even.

'It takes two or three years to look really good and it's quite a lot of work,' says Simon Hopkinson. 'Otherwise herb gardens, whether they're paved or just borders, are quite easy. They need keeping under control in May and June,

but after that the weeds can't compete any longer. So all you need to do is to cut back the herbs during winter.'

For the Hopkinsons, the original romantic impulse to sell up and get out of London has turned into a viable business. 'It doesn't matter where you run to, you have got to pay the bill,' says Simon Hopkinson. 'A business sense has to override everything else if you are to be successful. But both of us also have to be involved in something we enjoy. Herbs still give us that enjoyment. I still get a thrill from what you can do with them and the wonderful effects you can achieve with them in a garden.'

● **A culinary herb garden (left) with blue borage, orange marigolds and tree onions, and (below) rosemary and cotton lavender.**

As growers of herbs, I suppose it is only natural that we should want to use them in garden designs. People approach us having decided that they want a herb garden – this is usually a small area of an existing garden which they see as being ideal for herbs. It is seldom that we are asked to design the entire garden.

Herbs are two-dimensional – visually attractive as many plants are, but with the added magic of soft colours and contrasting foliage and the wonderful scents of the leaves and flowers. Herbs are to be used in every sense – the plants should be touched, used in cooking, walked on or brushed against, or cut for use in the house.

To design a herb garden successfully is quite difficult for it is one thing to draw up a plan on paper but quite another to understand what will happen after a couple of years. Herbs make a garden special – they appeal to people who like a challenge as well as enjoy letting nature take its own course; herbs always look thier best in the summer with little showing in the winter months – to watch an angelica or fennel growing from nothing to 6ft in a few weeks still gives us a thrill especially when it seeds itself around the place setting up new combinations of plants, some to be hoed out and others left to form new groups. (It's sort of working with nature!)

Simon Hopkinson

Further Information

John Sales

The National Trust, 36 Queen Anne's Gate, London SW1 9AS.

Mark Rumary

A catalogue is available from Notcutts Nurseries, Woodbridge, Suffolk. Notcutts also offer Garden-by-Post and Plant-a-Plan services – information from the nursery.

Brochures on paving are available from Marshalls Mono Limited, Southowram, Halifax, HX3 9SY, and Blanc de Bierges, Eastrea Road, Whittlesea, Peterborough, PE7 2AG.

Iris Strachan

National Council for the Conservation of Plants and Gardens, Wisley Gardens, near Woking, Surrey GU23 6QB.

Rare plants are available from Plants from the Past, 1 North Street, Belhaven, Dunbar. Open March to September from 10am to 5pm.

A plant list is available from Northumbria Nurseries, Castle Gardens, Ford, Berwick-on-Tweed, Northumberland. The Bell's Whisky Heather Collection can be seen at Cherrybank Gardens, Cherrybank, Perth.

Myles Challis

A catalogue of tropical and sub-tropical plants is available from Anmore Exotics, The George Staunton Estate, Petersfield Road, Havant, Hampshire PO9 5HB.

A catalogue of hardy palms is available from the Palm Farm, Thornton Hall Gardens, Ulceby, South Humberside. DN39 6XF.

The Exotic Garden, Myles Challis, Fourth Estate.
The Plant Finder, edited by Tony Lord, Moorland Publishing.

Arabella Lennox-Boyd

Traditional English Gardens, Arabella Lennox-Boyd and Clay Perry, Weidenfeld.

Julian Treyer-Evans

Details of mature shrubs and trees for an instant garden are available from Squires garden centres, Garden Store Centres, and Notcutts Nurseries, Woodbridge, Suffolk.

Susan Gernaey

A catalogue of conservatory plants is available from Read's Nursery, Hales Hall, Loddon, Norfolk.

Anthony du Gard Pasley

Planning and planting courses are run by The English Gardening School, Chelsea Physic Garden, 66 Royal Hospital Road, London SW3 4HS.

The English Gardening School – Anthony du Gard Pasley and Rosemary Alexander, Michael Joseph.

Michael Balston

Michael Balston's garden ornaments are available from The Landscape Ornament Company, Voysey House, Barley Mow Passage, London W4 4PN.

The Well Furnished Garden, Michael Balston, Mitchell Beazley.

John Brookes

Clock House School of Garden Design, Denmans Garden, Fontwell, near Arundel, West Sussex.

The New Small Garden Book, John Brookes, Dorling Kindersley
The Garden Book, John Brookes, Dorling Kindersley.
The Indoor Garden Book, John Brookes, Dorling Kindersley.
The Country Garden, John Brookes, Dorling Kindersley.
The Gardener's Index of Plants and Flowers, John Brookes and Kenneth Beckett, Dorling Kindersley.
The Pocket Encyclopaedia of House-plants, contributing editor John Brookes, Dorling Kindersley.

Anthony Paul

Water plants can be obtained from Stapeley Water Gardens, Stapeley, Nantwich, Cheshire CW5 7LH.

Hot tubs are available from Hot Tubs Limited, Wisborough Green, West Sussex.

The Garden Design Book, Anthony Paul and Yvonne Rees, Collins.

Simon and Judith Hopkinson

Catalogue and plant list available from Hollington Nursery, Woolton Hill, Newbury, Berkshire. Open 10am to 5.30pm; 10am to 5pm Sundays and Bank Holidays.

The Herb Society, 77 St Peters Street, London SW1

Herbs, Simon and Judith Hopkinson, Century Hutchinson.

Fast growing plants to hide eyesores

Chamaecyparis. *Chamaecyparis lawsoniana* is a fast growing conifer which puts on about 50 centimetres a year. It will grow at least 12 metres high with a spread of about 3 metres unless it is cut back. It can be planted as a large tree to blot out an unpleasant landscape but will need space. It makes rather a thick hedge.

Clematis. *Clematis montana* will climb 12 metres high and bear a mass of flowers each May. It is useful for smothering an ugly wall or for climbing up an unattractive tree. Unfortunately it loses its leaves in winter.

● **All varieties of honeysuckle, or *Lonicera*, are useful for covering up.**

Lonicera. Eyesores like oil tanks or old sheds can be covered up with honeysuckle. Japanese honeysuckle is a strong growing variety with evergreen leaves useful for covering up garden eyesores with fragrant yellow flowers from July onwards. *Lonicera japonica* 'Aureoreticulata' is its variegated form. *Lonicera x americana* has pink and white flowers in a spectacular display during June and July.

Plants for shade

All these plants will grow in semi-shade and some will survive in deep shade. A few of them will survive deep shade and dry conditions. Some are to be found in ordinary garden centres; others will need ordering from mail order specialists. If yours is a difficult garden, it is well worth making sure you get the best variety, not just the one that the local garden centre has in stock.

Annuals and biennials

Digitalis. The common wild foxglove, *Digitalis purpurea,* is found in dappled shade at the edge of woodland. Seed firms sell cultivated varieties in colours ranging from cream through pink to purple, and ranging in size from giant to dwarf. Foxgloves self-seed themselves through the garden but most of the garden varieties seed back to the original wild flower. The yellow foxglove, *Digitalis grandiflora,* a perennial which grows to 60 centimetres and *Digitalis lutea* which reaches 1 metre, can be found in good nurseries. The common foxglove and its relations are biennial, flowering in their second year. Grown in a mass, the ordinary wild foxglove makes an impressive show.

Impatiens. Busy Lizzies, or *Impatiens walleriana*, are the ideal bedding plant to lighten up a shady garden. Avoid the variegated leaved varieties if you are planting in deep shade. Sown from seed and bedded out in early July, busy Lizzies survive where other bedding plants would die. The white flowered varieties glow in dark corners of the garden – try the F1 hybrid 'Super Elfin White'.

Lunaria. A biennial plant, honesty or *Lunaria biennis* puts up its rich purple flowers in April to June of the second year.

These grow up to 75 centimetres high and are followed by purplish flat seed cases which are beautiful when dried. They can also be split to reveal shining silver membranes, which, since they look like the moon, give the plant its Latin name. Honesty will grow happily in partial shade and self-seeds round the garden. There is also a white flowered variety called 'Alba' and a form 'Variegata' with spectacular white variegated leaves which grows true to seed. Both purple flowered and white flowered variegated forms exist though the latter is rare.

Perennials and bulbs

Ajuga. Commonly known as bugle, this is a low hardy perennial which will tolerate and grow both in shade and sun. It is originally a woodland plant and is often used as ground cover for shady spots, though in deep shade its foliage may lose its colouring. *Ajuga reptans* 'Burgundy Glow' has wine-red leaves with light blue flower spikes 10 centimetres high. *Ajuga reptans* 'Braunherz' has purple-bronze leaves with deep blue flower spikes 15 centimetres high, while the 'Purpurea' variety has deep blue flowers 10 centimetres high with reddish-purple leaves. The variegated form 'Variegata' is slower growing with cream and light green leaves, with blue flowers 10 centimetres high.

Alchemilla. Its common name is Lady's mantle and it is a tough hardy perennial which will grow in almost all conditions. Its attractive foliage glistens with raindrops and it bears green-yellow flowers on loose floppy sprays from June to August. *Alchemilla mollis,* the most common variety, seeds itself round the garden with flower sprays reaching 45 centimetres. Not only is it useful for flower arrangers but it will even grow in dry shade. *Alchemilla alpina* is a smaller silvery plant with flower sprays only 15 centimetres high. *Alchemilla ellenbeckii*, even smaller at 10 centimetres, has been described as the ideal ground coverer.

Asperula.
Sweet woodruff, or *Asperula odorata* (sometimes also called *Galium odoratum*), thrives in damp shady places. It makes good ground cover about 15 centimetres high under shrubs. In early summer it has small white flowers but its leaves need drying to release their fragrance of new mown hay. The Elizabethans valued it as a strewing herb. As a native plant it would be suitable for a wildlife garden.

Bergenia.
Known as Elephant's ears, these tough perennials with evergreen foliage will grow almost anywhere. Cultivars come in a range of whites, pinks and reds. *Bergenia* 'Abendglut' or 'Evening Glow' combines vivid rose red flower heads 30 centimetres high in March with foliage that turns deep red in winter. *Bergenia* 'Ballawley'' is a larger hybrid, growing up to 60 centimetres with rose red flowers and green leaves that turn bronze in the frost. *Bergenia* 'Bressingham White' sends up white flowers 80 centimetres high, while 'Bressingham Salmon' has smaller pink flowers 25 centimetres tall. A good plant as ground cover for a difficult part of the garden, *Bergenia* will grow in dry shade.

Euphorbia.
From the spurge family come two perennial plants that will grow in shade. *Euphorbia cyparissias* is a ground cover plant with lime flowerheads in early summer growing 30 centimetres. *Euphorbia robbiae* is a handsome taller plant with sulphur yellow flowerheads growing 45 centimetres high. Its deep green foliage with leaves in a rosette shape takes up quite a lot of space. This is a good plant to fill up a difficult corner. The plants have a milky sap to which some people may be allergic.

Fatshedera.
Fatshedera lizei is a hybrid between an ivy and a *Fatsia japonica* which will grow in dry shade but needs support if it is to stay upright. Often used as ground cover tumbling down a bank, it grows 1.5 to 2.5 metres high. A variegated form, *Fatshedera lizei* 'Variegata' has ivy shaped leaves edged with cream.

Ferns.
Ferns thrive in shade but only if the soil is moist. Among our native species is the hart's tongue fern, *Asplenium scolopendrium*, which would be useful for a wildlife garden. So would some of the different *Dryopteris* species native to this country. There are a confusing number of different ferns and the best place for information is a catalogue from a specialist nursery.

Hedera.
The many varieties of ivy with its hardy evergreen leaves make perfect climbing plants for shaded walls and also good ground cover for dry shade. There are three different species involved – *Hedera canariensis* and *Hedera colchica* both have large glossy leaves. Our native ivy is *Hedera helix*, with its smaller leaf. There are so many different cultivated varieties that it is difficult to know which to single out. 'Goldheart' has dark green leaves with a golden heart shaped centre: 'Silver

● *Helleborus niger*, the Christmas rose. Hellebores will add interest to the winter or early spring garden, and will self-seed.

Queen' has a cream silvery variegation. A rare variety is Poet's ivy, *Helix poetica* 'Arborea', grown like a bush with yellow-orange berries.

Helleborus.
These are plants for bringing interest to the winter or early spring garden. *Helleborus foetidus*, known as stinking hellebore, has dark green architectural foliage and pale green flowers growing 60 centimetres high from January onwards. A really useful perennial plant for dark corners it will survive in dry shade. It will seed itself round the garden. *Helleborus lividus corsicus* has a wider leaf and apple green flowers growing 60 centimetres high. More striking as a garden plant, it is not as tough as its native cousin and while it likes a shady spot, cannot tolerate dry shade. Both the Christmas rose, *Helleborus niger*, with its white flowers 30 centimetres high in January, and the Lenten rose, *Helleborus orientalis*, with purplish flowers from February, prefer semi-shade but need a soil with plenty of humus. These interbreed and will self-seed through the garden.

Iris. Stinking iris, the roast beef plant (named after the smell of its leaves) or *Iris foetidissima* is a native woodland plant which will grow in dry deep shade. It has small delicate purple flowers 50 centimetres high in June, followed in autumn by orange berried seedheads much loved by flower arrangers for dried flower arrangements. A really useful plant for difficult dark corners, since its leaves give architectural interest throughout the year. There is a yellow flowered variety 'Citrina'. *Iris foetidissima* 'Variegata' keeps its variegated marking on the foliage in semi-shade, growing 45 centimetres high, but takes longer to establish itself than the non-variegated kind and is slow to flower in deep shade.

Lamium. This is the dead nettle family of which yellow archangel, or *Lamium galeobdolon*, with its yellow flowers, will grow 20 to 25 centimetres high, and will flourish in shade. It comes in several variegated forms – 'Herman's Pride', 'Silver Carpet' or 'Variegata'. *Lamium maculatum*, a similar plant but low growing at only 10 centimetres also comes in different variegated forms. 'Aureum', 'Beacon Silver', and 'Chequers' are some of them. Their only disadvantage is that like other ground cover plants, they may be difficult to eradicate.

Liriope. Another architectural plant useful as ground cover in semi-shade, *Liriope muscari*, or lily turf, has dark spiky foliage and autumn flowering violet spikes 30 centimetres high looking rather like tall grape hyacinths. It will tolerate dry conditions.

Lonicera. The honeysuckles will flourish even in shade. The native variety, *Lonicera periclymenum*, has cream orange tinted flowers from June to October followed by red berries. Cultivated varieties tend to flower more continuously through the summer.

Melissa. An apothecary's herb, balm or *Melissa officinalis* grows up to 60 centimetres high with lemon scented leaves and tiny white flowers. Bees love it and it is one of the few herbs that can survive in semi-shade. There are two variegated forms – 'Aurea' with gold leaves and 'Variegata' with gold and green leaves.

Polygonatum. Soloman's seal or *Polygonatum multiflorum* is one of our native woodland plants. Growing 75 centimetres high it has arching sprays of pendant bell-like white flowers and can survive in dry shade, though it dislikes its rhizomes being disturbed. There are several cultivated varieties including a variegated form 'Variegatum' growing 60 centimetes high and a taller one 100 centimetres high called *Polygonatum giganteum* or *japonicum*.

Pulmonaria. The lungwort, *Pulmonaria officinalis*, with spotted leaves and blue-pink bell-shaped flowers, is a native species growing to 40 centimetres in shady places. It would thus be suitable for a wildlife garden. There are many cultivated varieties of pulmonaria including *Pulmonaria saccharata* 'Sissinghurst white' with green leaves and white flowers 25 centimetres high, as well as *Pulmonaria saccharata* 'Highdown' with blue flowers 30 centimetres high. 'Margery Fish' is a variety of the same plant with silver and green variegated leaves and pink to blue flowers growing 25 centimetres which is described as 'ideal in dry shade'. 'Argentea' is another form, this time with wholly silvered leaves.

Tiarella. The low growing *Tiarella collina* with soft green foliage and creamy white flower sprays 30 centimetres high in early summer will thrive in shady places and even survive in dry shade. Other possibilities are *Tiarella cordifolia* with pointed green leaves and cream white flower spikes 25 centimetres high, and *Tiarella wherryi* with golden green foliage and cream white flower spikes 25 centimetres high.

Viola. *Viola labradorica* could be a pest in the garden, were it not so attractive with its dark purple leaves and lighter coloured blue flowers. It spreads by roots as well as self-seeding. Low growing only 15 centimetres high, it is useful in dry shade.

Shrubs and trees

Aucuba. Spotted laurel or *Aucuba japonica* was a great favourite of the Victorians with its decorative leaves and scarlet berries. It will survive in semi-shade. A variety called 'Rozannie' is self fertile and will therefore produce berries when only a single plant is grown.

Buxus. Common box or *Buxus sempervirens* is an undervalued shrub in the garden. Not only can it be used for topiary and for hedging but it is useful for mazes or knot gardens. It is a useful backbone evergreen for the shady garden, growing up to 3 metres high but kept smaller by pruning. There are two variegated forms – 'Aureovariegata' with gold variegated leaves and 'Elegantissima' with silver edged leaves.

Cornus. Commonly called dogwood, these shrubs will grow in light shade but like wet conditions. There are a wide range of cultivars with differently coloured foliage. *Cornus alba sibirica*, the Westonbirt dogwood, with beautiful red stems will survive in deep shade.

Eunonymus. This family includes a group of low growing shrubs, *Eunonymus fortunei*, that will grow in shade and are useful for ground cover. The variety 'Emerald 'n Gold' grows up to 30 centimetres with green, gold and pink tinged leaves. 'Silver Queen' with white and green leaves can grow up to 3 metres against a wall, but can also be used as ground cover since it has a trailing habit. It's useful for bringing light into dark places. It survives even dry shade. For a small tree growing up to 2.5 metres try *Eunonymus europaeus* 'Red Cascade', a cultivated variety of the native spindle tree. It has good autumn colouring but is remarkable for its orange-red fruits and will survive deep shade.

Hypericum. *Hypericum androsaemum* is a bushy shrub which will grow to 60 centimetres in semi-shade and flowers from June to August with yellow flowers that turn into black berries. There is a variegated cultivar 'Variegata' or 'Mrs Gladis Brabazon' with leaves splashed pink and white.

Prunus. There are two plants of this family, which are commonly known as laurels. *Prunus laurocerasus*, the common laurel, grows up to 4.5 metres and will survive in quite dark shade. Its April flowers are succeeded by red berries, turning black when ripe. *Prunus lusitanica*, known as the Portuguese Laurel, has slender creamy white flowers in June and grows up to 4.5 metres high.

Sambucus. The ordinary elder bush, *Sambucus nigra*, is a rampant plant which will grow almost anywhere. There are also ornamental varieties with interesting foliage useful for shady gardens with enough space. 'Aureomarginata' has dark green leaves with a yellow margin and grows to 2 metres. 'Purpurea' has purple black leaves and grows to 2.5 metres.

Skimmia. This family of evergreen shrubs with fragrant flowers needs both a male and female plant, if the females are to produce the subsequent red berries. *Skimmia japonica* grows slowly up to 1.5 metres high with fragrant flowers in April succeeded by scarlet berries in September. The variety 'Reevesiana', growing up to 40 centimetres, is self-fertile and should therefore produce berries if planted singly.

Plants for shape

Annuals and biennials

Eryngium. *Eryngium giganteum*, a large biennial sea holly growing more than 1 metre high, has been nicknamed Miss Willmott's ghost because the famous gardener used to sprinkle its seeds in the border of favoured friends. Its flowerheads with wide ruff of spiny bracts surrounding them make a striking feature in a herbaceous border.

Nicotiana. *Nicotiana Sylvestris* is an Argentinian tobacco plant growing 1.5 metres high with a cluster of long white trumpets which have a delicious fragrance. Its large leaves at the base of the plant have a spread of 60 centimetres so this is not a bedding plant for a small garden.

Perennials

Acanthus. *Acanthus spinosus*, commonly called bear's breeches, has architectural deep-cut foliage and puts up white and purple flower spikes up to 1.2 metres high. This is an aggressive plant which will take out the weaker competition so is best grown in a patch on its own.

Crambe. A giant seakale, *Crambe cordifolia* grows up to 3 metres high and wide with a mass of tiny white flowers in June growing out of its dark green foliage. It needs space to do its own thing and is not suitable for the small garden.

Eryngium. There are several different perennial sea hollies which do best in sunny conditions and add architectural interest in the smaller garden. Flower arrangers like their spiky flowerheads and both flowers and foliage make interesting shapes. *Eryngium x oliverianum* grows 50 centimetres high with spiny blue foliage and blue flowerheads.

Hosta. For smaller gardens, hostas which come in all sizes can produce an architectural effect. Try *Hosta sieboldiana* with blue-green leaves which grows up to 50 centimetres high.

Onopordum. *Onopordum acanthium*, known as Scotch thistle, is a spectacular border plant growing up to 1.5 metres high with striking grey foliage.

Phormium. *Phormium tenax*, or New Zealand flax, is a spiky plant which comes in various different coloured varieties. Grown for its shape rather than its flowerheads, which grow up to 3 metres high, the coloured-leaved varieties need some protection from frost.

Shrubs and trees

Fatsia. *Fatsia japonica* is a shrub, growing 2.5 to 4.5 metres high, which will thrive in semi-shade. Its dark green glossy leaves and globular creamy flowers in autumn make it a striking plant for a town garden.

Juniper. Juniper now comes in all kinds of shapes, sizes and colours. It's worth getting a specialist catalogue and buying by mail order rather than simply buying what is in your local garden centre. One of the best known varieties is *Juniperus scopulorum* 'Skyrocket', a grey blue pencil-shaped tree growing up to 3 metres high.

Mahonia. Growing up to 3 metres with a spread of about 2.5 metres, *Mahonia x* 'Charity' has sprays of yellow flowers in early spring which smell of lily of the valley and are followed by blue-black berries.

Plants for wildlife

This is not an exhaustive list. Those who want a proper wildlife garden would do well to go to a specialist seed company. These are just a few of the wild flowers which earn their place among the cultivated varieties for their charm and beauty.

Annuals and biennials

Digitalis. The common wild foxglove, *Digitalis purpurea,* is found in dappled shade at the edge of the wood and is a good plant for a wild garden. Foxgloves self-seed themselves through the garden. The common foxglove and its relations are biennial, flowering in their second year. Grown in a mass, the ordinarily wild foxglove makes an impressive show.

● **The common foxglove, *Digitalis purpurea*, grows in dappled shade and is a good plant for a wild garden.**

Lunaria. A biennial plant, honesty or *Lunaria biennis* puts up its rich purple flowers in April to June of the second year. These grow up to 75 centimetres high and are followed by purplish flat seed cases which are beautiful dried. They can also be split to reveal shining silver membranes, which, since they look like the moon, give the plant its Latin name. Honesty will grow happily in partial shade and self-seeds round the garden. It provides food for the orange-tip butterfly and its caterpillars.

Perennials

Asperula. Sweet woodruff, or *Asperula odorata* (sometimes also called *Galium odoratum*), thrives in damp shady places. It makes a good ground cover about 15 centimetres high under shrubs. In early summer it has small white flowers but its leaves need drying to release their fragrance of new mown hay.

Aquilegia. The cottage garden favourite columbine or granny's bonnet, *Aquilegia vulgaris,* is one of our native species. With purple, pink or white flowers it grows up to 60 centimetres high.

Colchicum. The autumn crocus, *Colchicum autumnale,* also known as naked ladies or meadow saffron, puts up a naked flowerhead up to 30 centimetres high in September, then its leaves appear in spring. Useful for naturalising or for providing a succession of blooms in the herbaceous border.

Convallaria. Lily of the valley, *Convallaria majalis,* is a woodland plant which spreads vigorously. Its bell-shaped flowers, no more than 15 centimetres, in loose spikes in late spring and early summer, have a delicious fragrance. It is a plant which will survive in dry shade.

Endymion. The common bluebell, *Endymion nonscriptus,* can be used for ground cover under trees. In early summer woods are a carpet of blue. Its only disadvantage is the messy pulp of foliage as it dies down. Easy to naturalise but difficult to eradicate.

● ***Endymion*, or the common bluebell.**

Geranium. These are the cranes-bill plants, the true perennial geraniums among which are so many beautiful flowers for the herbacious border. Meadow cranes-bill, *Geranium pratense,* one of our wild flowers, makes a lovely border flower with its blue flowers growing up to 60 centimetres high. It will seed itself through the border given the chance. It can also be grown as a grassland plant.

Inula. Elecampane, or *Inula helenium,* is often sold as a medicinal herb. A tall plant with yellow daisy-like flowers it can grow up to 3 metres high. It needs plenty of room in the flower border but is one of the more spectacular flowers of our native species.

Iris. Stinking iris, the roast beef plant (named after the smell of its leaves) or *Iris* *foetidissima* is a native woodland plant which will grow in dry deep shade. It has small delicate purple flowers 50 centimetres high in June, followed in autumn by orange berried seedheads much loved by flower arrangers for dried flower arrangements. A really useful plant for difficult dark corners, since its leaves give interest throughout the year.

● **The stinking iris, or *Iris foetidissima***

Lamium. This is the dead nettle family of which yellow archangel, or *Lamium galeobdolon,* with its yellow flowers, would make a good plant for a wildlife garden. Growing 20 to 25 centimetres high, it will flourish even in shade.

Leucanthemum. Ox-eyed daisy, *Leucanthemum vulgare,* grows up to 45 centimetres high with a striking daisy flower from May to September. It is a plant for grassy places in full sun.

Primula. The common primrose, *Primula vulgaris,* and the cowslip, *Primula veris,* are lovely spring flowers and if they are happy will self-seed themselves round the garden. The cowslip prefers limey soil.

● **The common primrose, *primula vulgaris*, is a welcome sight in spring. It will seed itself around the garden.**

Pulmonaria. Lungwort, *Pulmonaria officinalis,* with spotted leaves and blue-pink bell-shaped flowers, is a native species growing to 40 centimetres in shady places. It would thus be suitable for a wildlife garden.

Pulsatilla. The Pasque flower or *Pulsatilla vulgaris* earns its place in any rock garden with its feathery foliage and rich purple flowers about 28 centimetres high, followed by attractive seedheads.

Vinca. The periwinkle is a native plant with blue flowers in early spring above leathery leafy stems. A good choice for a wildlife garden, there are two native species, the lesser periwinkle, *Vinca minor,* and the greater periwinkle, *Vinca major.* Both make good ground cover and survive in dry shade.

Shrubs

Cornus. Commonly called dogwood, these shrubs will grow in light shade but like wet conditions. There are a wide range of cultivars with differently coloured foliage. Two of the dogwoods – *Cornus mas* and *Cornus sanguinea* are native shrubs and can be planted in wildlife gardens.

Cotoneaster. The best known variety is *Cotoneaster horizontalis,* a herring-bone shaped shrub which grows up walls about 60 centimetres high or hugs the ground horizontally. It is happy in semi-shade. With tiny pink flowers much loved by bees in late spring, and red berries appreciated in winter by hungry thrushes, it has an important place in the wildlife garden.

Eunonymus. The ordinary native spindle growing up to 6 metres is a woodland shrub with striking bright coral pink berries – a good choice for a wildlife garden.

Sorbus. Mountain ash or rowan, *Sorbus aucuparia,* provides berries for birds and good autumn colouring on its leaves as well as creamy white flowers in summer for the gardener. It reaches a height of 7 metres or more.

Taxus. The seeds inside the yew berries are poisonous for humans and the foliage will poison farm animals, so yew should only be used for hedging in gardens where there are neither children nor neighbouring farm animals. Yew hedges have a reputation of being slow growing but are worth waiting for.